VILLAGE
YORKSHIRE

VILLAGE
YORKSHIRE

*A pilgrimage through history
and the Broad Acres*

MAURICE COLBECK

Photography by Fred Spencer

B.T. BATSFORD LTD · LONDON

By the same author:

Yorkshire
Yorkshire Historymakers
Queer Folk
Yorkshire Laughter
Yorkshire: the Dales
Yorkshire Moorlands
And others

For Brenda

First published 1987

ISBN 0 7134 5032 0

Typeset by Servis Filmsetting Ltd, Manchester
and printed by
Butler & Tanner Ltd
Frome, Somerset
for the publishers
B.T. Batsford Ltd
4 Fitzhardinge Street
London W1H 0AH

CONTENTS

LIST OF ILLUSTRATIONS

Between pages 96 and 97

FOREWORD

This being a personal appreciation of the village wealth of the Ridings, there are bound to be omissions, more or less reprehensible depending on the reader's predilections. For these I can only apologize, as I do for any inaccuracies, misquotations, unwitting infringements, the necessary restatement of certain facts mentioned in my earlier books, or other sins that beset anyone rash enough to be an author.

I am grateful to Fred Spencer for his fine photography and to my innumerable informants including previous writers (most of whom are mentioned in the Bibliography). I must also thank Peggy Hewitt and Springfield Books for permission to quote from *These Lonely Mountains*, and Peter Winstone for allowing me to use some lines from *The Story of the Witch of Clapham*. A few passages in the pages that follow have appeared in the magazine *Yorkshire Life*. My thanks are also due to Constance Drake for permission to quote from *The Pace Egg*, of which her father, H.W. Harwood, and F.H. Marsden were joint authors.

My debt to my wife is acknowledged, inadequately, in the dedication.

County Map

N.B. Only for use in locating places described in this book.

Too rich to lose, too rare to spoil

Why write about villages? It would be easy to offer the platitude that 'we are all villagers at heart' – except that it isn't true: there are those for whom the only desirable environment is a city, and the bigger the better.

Even so, I venture to believe that would-be denizens of a human anthill are in a minority and that most of us, given the choice, would opt for life in the country. And unless you are a hermit by temperament, that usually means life in a village.

Much depends on age, perhaps. If you were born in a village you are more likely to have spent your early years wanting nothing so much as to escape from it to what you see as the wider world beyond. But if you have not had that advantage – and I believe it usually is an advantage, especially if it includes a village school education – you will probably find in later life a hankering to return to roots that were put down only in dreams.

We tend to idealize the village as the home of peace and beauty, of quaint, lovable characters, of venerable cottages, inns and churches embodying a community that in its customs, work and play perpetuates the best qualities of our national life. Not for nothing is one of the longest-running radio programmes based on a fictitious village named Ambridge. The Archers have entered so deeply into our communal psyche that they have taken on a vivid life of their own. And this is evidenced not only by the endearingly naive souls who seem unable or unwilling to accept that the personalities on whom they eavesdrop so avidly have no existence outside a script-writer's imagination: indeed, the village of Ambridge has become so real that learned tomes on its 'local history' are produced, including genealogies of its leading worthies.

The village generally, it seems, has become a Never-Never Land, where Everyone is Somebody and not just another two-legged ant scurrying to catch the 8.15. What a contrast is the scene at Egton Bridge on the North York Moors, when the Old Gooseberry Society holds its annual show; where every man is only as good as his berries, grown according to his most secret stratagems of pruning, watering and manuring. Ah, here, we feel, people know how to live.

But am I being too analytical, even cynical? Is not the real appeal of village life a matter of peace and quiet in the countryside, of well nourished traditions, of the 'caring' community *par excellence*, where nobody can fall upon hard times without his plight attracting notice; where it would be impossible and unthinkable for an old man or woman to die alone in a bed-sit? Yet there may be those who claim that the very 'caringness' of village life denies them privacy; that in the real-life Ambridges, just as in the radio version, everybody knows your business. If so, that is surely preferable to the growing isolation of modern urban life. In the towns and cities, the old 'street' communities seem to be outstripped by 'progress', while village life becomes, if anything, less insular, more tolerant and more accepting of the incomers and visitors, strange as their behaviour may sometimes be.

On the whole, that is. For there are doubtless those who see the 'comers-in' from the towns and cities as restless busybodies who cannot leave the indigenous population in peace, who dragoon others into unwanted activity; who send up property values and buy up as holiday homes the cottage which might otherwise provide homes for young village folk forced by financial necessity to emigrate to the towns and cities. That school of thought exists, yet even what might be considered the village diehards are often warm in their appreciation of the benefits brought by the comers-in. Country folk are not the stick-in-the-muds townies often suppose. Their close contact with the basic realities of life makes them aware that change is inevitable, that some changes are desirable and that others are long overdue.

For village life is not a 'settled state'; it never was, though the inhabitants of Wharram Percy on the East Yorkshire Wolds no doubt regarded change as unthinkable. They were not to know that the men who owned the land whose crops they harvested year after year would suddenly be dazzled by the prospect of the wealth to be made by turning their land over to sheep; would evict the ploughman and his family, leaving their homes and cattle sheds to slow decay. Today, only a crumbling church and a floating population of archaeologists remain. And Wharram Percy is only one abandoned village in over a hundred in the East Riding alone.

While some villages die, others are born . . . I think of New Earswick near York, where early this century Joseph Rowntree of the chocolate company founded a trust to provide a model village. Thus was Quaker social conscience allied with success in business to the benefit of the 'persons with small incomes' who were the original residents. A similar combination of industry and philanthropy led to the founding of a West Riding model village, Saltaire, by the Nonconformist cloth manufacturer Sir Titus Salt, at one time owner of the biggest factory in the world. Saltaire, which still stands beside the Aire, almost in Bradford, retains a pleasant, half-rural air, though it doubtless failed to please all those favoured to be residents: it had everything, you see, school, hospital, library – except a pub.

Such recent and purpose-built villages may not enshrine the traditions of centuries in the way that Kilburn or Goathland, Bainbridge or Reeth enshrine them, but their inhabitants display what for me is the essential quality of village life, the deep, protective love of most villagers for the community they see as a trust, both in terms of its fabric and what would once have been called its 'souls'. Indeed, among older villagers the departure of a well-loved son or daughter of the village for other stonier fields is seen as almost a case for mourning. 'When is 'e comin' 'ome?' the wife of a friend of mine is lugubriously asked whenever she meets one ancient from her husband's native Wharfedale.

Since each village has its peculiar flavour, I can imagine worse fates than an eternity of village tasting; whilst to be admitted to the inner circle – or one of them – of village life is a privilege not lightly to be esteemed.

For instance, many years ago, staying in a village pub in Wensleydale I had my introduction to the mysteries of the spirit world – if such it was. In association with favoured regulars, mine hostess presided at a table around which we sat with fingers resting on an upturned tumbler which would whizz about the table spelling out messages and answering questions often with astonishing accuracy. As the onlooking wise-acres from the bar would observe, 'It's queer – it is that!' And a kind of Greek chorus of support would solemnly agree: 'You're right there, Joe. It's *queer!*'

My subject is the villages of Yorkshire. Other counties have their village gems which inevitably some would consider superior to our home-grown versions. Where the Broad Acres excel, as always, is in the variety on offer. For where else but in Yorkshire could you find not only fishing villages like Staithes and Robin Hood's Bay, but the half-industrialized villages of the Pennines or South Yorkshire; or stone-built hamlets which seem to have sprung from the very fabric of the Dales or the softer, warmer-coloured eastern moorlands.

My fear is that the growth of tourism and the increasing awareness of village dwellers of the richness beneath their feet may foster a cynical commercialism. Ryedale in North Yorkshire receives much attention in the pages that follow – 'there are few pleasanter areas in England', I once wrote, 'a fact which, despite the efforts of the local authority and the Yorkshire and Humberside Tourist Board, is known to comparatively few tourists ...' Perhaps I spoke too soon!

For only today I read: 'Ryedale launches village tourism campaign ... the aim is to create and support jobs in the countryside, and to boost rural prosperity but without causing local congestion or putting the environment at risk.' It sounds laudable and responsible enough, though I must admit that the launch of a 'most tourist-minded village' award awakens some misgivings.

Yet what are the alternatives? Villages are living organisms, not communities preserved in amber. If their survival depends on change, then surely change is preferable to a deadly harvest of deserted villages like those on the Wolds that failed to find a new rôle when farming patterns changed.

Perhaps the new village rôle is to be a green, recreational oasis where traditional observances, vernacular architecture, time-honoured crafts and sports can survive without forcing, can even flourish easily and naturally to the great benefit of visitor and resident alike. Already in Ryedale the Folk Museum at Hutton le Hole recreates with great enjoyment the delights of bygone midsummers.

Such campaigns as that recently announced in Ryedale and said to be 'unique in Britain', need to be promoted with the sensitivity born of affection. Given that, they could lead the way in awakening the whole of Britain to a realization that the village is a treasure too rich to lose, too rare to spoil.

1

In at the dark end

A TREASURE HUNT FROM SHEFFIELD TO AIREDALE

Whoever first called Sheffield 'a dark picture in a frame of gold' conferred an inestimable favour on Yorkshire's steel metropolis by giving it something to live down. And this, Sheffield has been successfully doing ever since.

No longer dark, with city-centre gardens and a smug delight in the purity of its air, the city has become almost a snob about its proximity to the Peak District, taking a rather superior and distanced view of those not-too-salubrious parts of Yorkshire which impinge on its northern boundary.

Admittedly, the Derbyshire villages which are so much nearer Sheffield than are the Dales or the North York Moors have a deal more charm than some of Sheffield's nearer neighbours; but even the most industrial areas of Yorkshire have never lacked islands of rural, or near rural, delight. Within the city of Sheffield itself there is the Abbeydale Industrial Hamlet, hardly rural, but a marvellously preserved 'working model' of the old life of Sheffield, where tourists may see waterwheels, tilt-hammers and furnaces and the cottages built in the late eighteenth century to house workers at the Goddard family's Abbeydale scythe works. An example, this, of the industrial village which takes so many forms in Yorkshire, depending on whether the dominant industry be steel, coal or textiles.

The introduction of mechanical mowing and harvesting was to cause such a decline in the demand for scythes and sickles that production at Abbeydale ceased in 1933, though on summer weekends the old forges ring again as present-day craftsmen demonstrate ancient skills for the visitors.

Abbeydale brilliantly preserves the sort of industry carried out at numerous villages in the Sheffield area, which nevertheless retained a rural character until fairly recent times. Ford, Eckington, Hackenthorpe all 'lived by the scythe', frequently sharing the same grinding wheels. Norton, now truly a part of the city, was one of them. At heart it may well remain a village, but a vastly different village from that in which Francis Chantrey was born in 1781. His birthplace, Jordan-thorpe Farm, still stands – unmistakably – since a plaque to his memory was unveiled there in 1981, the two-hundredth anniversary of his birth.

Two centuries ago, few of his fellow villagers could have foreseen such future eminence for the dreamy, handsome youth who took milk on a donkey from his father's farm to sell in Sheffield. They may even have doubted his sanity as he passed them, whittling endlessly at a stick of wood. But those who saw the whittling eventually and magically emerge from his hands as a beautiful figurine, may well have guessed that Chantrey would some day be known as more than a farm boy delivering milk. Had he not had the good fortune to become apprenticed to a carver and gilder in Sheffield we might never have heard of him. But one thing led to another, and, through the good offices of the friends he so readily attracted, he was able to study portraiture and sculpture from professional artists without even leaving Sheffield. After a brief period of study at the Royal Academy he set up as a portrait painter in the northern city, where, later, he worked as a sculptor.

But London called him again. There, he won a competition for a statue of George III and from then on was constantly at work producing sculptures of the great and famous. The Duke of Wellington, William Wordsworth and Sir Walter Scott all sat for him, as well as four monarchs ranging from George III to Queen Victoria. He was knighted by William IV in 1835, but died only six years later.

He could have been buried in Westminster Abbey, but instead was laid to rest in the tomb he had himself prepared in the churchyard of St James's Church, his own parish church, in the area which was to become known as 'Chantreyland'.

A tablet in the church commemorates this most famous son of Norton who has been acknowledged as the best British sculptor of his time. But his abiding memorial is the bequest bearing his name, which he set up to provide for the purchase and encouragement of works by artists born in Britain.

At Norton today you may still see, at Jordanthorpe Farm, his sloping-ceilinged, low-raftered bedroom, lit by a little window with nine square panes. Opposite the church there is an obelisk to his memory. Fine houses, some of which he must have known, and old inns like the Bagshawe Arms and the Nailmaker's Arms add charm and dignity to this village on the edge of a city.

In 1981, the two-hundredth anniversary of his birth, Chantrey, remembered in a poem by Ebenezer Elliott, 'the Corn Law rhymer', as a milkboy 'calmly seated on his panniered ass', was the subject of celebrations not only in London and Sheffield but, chiefly, in his native village – which was surely what he would have wished.

The churchyard of St Nicholas, Bradfield, only a few miles west of the city, on the edge of the Bradfield Moors, affords a view of valley, hill and field that makes you pity the dead for being unable to see it. Beneath leaning tombstones they lie, enveloped in a silence broken only by the sigh of the wind in the trees and the bleat of a sheep.

Not that Martha Crookes, who departed this life in 1828, aged 37, would welcome your pity. From her gravestone she addresses us with the serenity of one reposing in absolute comfort:

> Go home, dear friends, and cease your tears.
> I must lie here till Christ appears.
> My debt is paid, my fate you see.
> Prepare yourselves to follow me.

I hope her confidence of lying undisturbed proved justified. That was not always the case, hence the fortress-like erection at the churchyard gate which was built in 1745 to house those watching out for body-snatchers. By today's standards it looks almost palatial, with enough chimneys to ensure that the watchmen kept a good deal warmer than their charges. Such lavish provision added an irony to the giant thermometer nearby, which recorded, when I was there last, the progress of a £75 000 appeal for the restoration of the magnificent fourteenth- and fifteenth-century church, gargoyled, pinnacled and castellated, whose fabric contains stonework from a still earlier building. Its registers date from 1538 and it takes proper pride in a sunken vestry with a fireplace, reputedly used as a resting place by monks from Ecclesfield after journeys across the moors.

The church is at the end of Towngate in High Bradfield, a vantage point for many centuries, as traces of prehistoric fortifications and a medieval motte and bailey bear witness. Later generations have used these valleys for storing the water which now adds a glinting beauty to the view while carrying sombre folk-memories of the dam-burst of 12 March 1864, which flooded villages around – Loxley, Little Matlock, Malin Bridge, Hillsborough – and cost 244 lives.

But things are ordered better now: boys and girls frolicked without fear by the beck in Low Bradfield and Sunday afternoon cricketers performed on their sloping field for an appreciative audience.

Opposite an elaborate Methodist chapel, almost hidden in trees, is its presumed forerunner, now the parish council offices. Built in 1817, its spare Georgian lines are mellowed by bright window boxes. Iron-framed lamps and more flowers in stone bowls flank its doorway. Just up the road is The Plough, sturdy in stone. The implement whose name it bears rests in a flower bed, discreetly chained to the pub wall. Thus Bradfield, quietly but firmly, retains its hold upon its past.

Several ancient villages accompany the course of the River Don as it winds through the country between Rotherham and Doncaster. Thrybergh has a Norman church with fragments of Saxon crosses. Hooton Roberts, a few miles along the A630, retains some Norman work in the church of St John the Baptist, which is reputedly the burial place of the Earl of Strafford, executed in 1641 by Parliament for his service to Charles I during what the Roundheads called 'the 11 years Tyranny'.

However, the noble earl has, in a sense, been resurrected. And all because tyranny of a different sort (or so some called it) no longer reigns. The 'tyranny' they complained of was the absence of a village pub, due to an edict by the lady of the manor, Violet Milner, who closed down the local hostelry 150 years ago to curtail her butler's boozing. She thus enforced sobriety on the rest of the village too. That is, until a few years ago when a new pub opened ... converted from the very manor house where Lady Violet used to live. The name of the new pub? The Earl of Strafford.

Just off the A1, Tickhill has a ruined castle, once licensed for tourneys by Richard I, and a fine church, St Mary the Virgin, whose tower rises 124 feet. Its nineteenth-century carillon enlivens the air at four-hourly intervals with a variety of tunes, changed daily from Sunday to Saturday. Despite the inevitable modern development and the near presence of heavy industry, the distant past has survived here with surprising tenacity; in one beautiful instance as a fourteenth-century Augustinian Friary, now a private house, on the Maltby road.

Conisbrough, too, has a castle, one of the chain of Norman strongholds hereabouts. But while Tickhill has retained much of its village ambience and only the fragmentary remains of its shell keep, Conisbrough's great Norman tower rises beside the Don in apparent defiance of the changes that have been seen in the township of steep streets and quaint corners at its feet. Not far away, colliery winding gear rises above the horizon, but these structures look spindly beside the stoutly buttressed, stately strength of the circular keep, one of the first in Britain, built about 1180 by Hamelin Plantagenet.

A few miles east of Tickhill on the A614, Austerfield seems hardly the place to associate with historic sea voyages. Yet here, at Austerfield Manor (now a private house with white walls and a red pantiled roof) was born William Bradford, one of the leaders of the Pilgrim Fathers who sailed in the *Mayflower* to seek religious freedom in the New World.

West of Conisbrough, the area between Rotherham, Barnsley and Doncaster is sprinkled with villages. The 'forgotten valley' it has been called, chosen in a BBC documentary to typify the 'growing difference between the north and the south of England', a heart-breaking example of the decline of an agricultural community. Wath-upon-Dearne may bear not the slightest resemblance to its namesakes in Nidderdale and Wensleydale, but it still rejoices in the name of village. Its long history, from Domesday times, has been linked with farming and – most notably during the last century or so – with coal-mining. And this last, combined with canal and railway development, gradually became dominant. But the tangible memories remain, like the old lock-up with two windowless cells below a constable's room, while in the church-yard of All Saints', which originated in Saxon times, there is buried among past notables George Naylor, whose fame is chronicled in a contemporary obituary.

George, who died in 1865 aged 73, was four feet seven inches short but he had 'the body of a stout strong man, with short crooked legs, scarcely a foot in length, and apparently far too weak to support the great burden nature had thrown upon them'. He earned his living as a rag and bone man with the help of a donkey 'as remarkable for its sagacity and docility as was its master for his strange form'. A burden perhaps even greater than George's 'strange form' was his persecution at the hands of crowds of village children who would provoke him to chase them. He never caught them but often fell flat on the ground in his efforts to do so, 'to the intense delight of the youngsters', records his obituarist.

However, 'he was good natured, and often made a feint of chasing the children to amuse them.' Poor George!

The A1, between Doncaster and Pontefract, traverses the sort of mixed countryside that most exemplifies the West Riding. To the outsider, who knows no more of Doncaster, Pontefract or Castleford than their names and vaguely associates those with engineering, coal mining or perhaps licorice, the area is often imagined as an industrial desert. Yet here may be found old villages sometimes far less spoilt than many in the well known tourist haunts.

One of them, Hooton Pagnell, with its grey stone, pantile-roofed houses terracing the hill, its hall, its green and butter cross, seems as secure and unchanging as any in the Dales, despite the effect on some buildings of subsidence from the tunnels that run below its pastures and cornfields from distant coalmines. Here, within two or three miles of 'typical' colliery towns, there exists a medieval-style stone farming village centring on its church and hall, with its fourteenth-century gatehouse dominant as a castle. There is even a dungeon, whose inmates' food was lowered to them on strings.

Here originated the famous Luttrell Psalter, now in the British Museum, which was commissioned by the third Sir George Luttrell, lord of the manor, in about 1340. Scenes of village life depicted therein include mummers, a comic wrestling match, villeins ploughing with oxen, a woman milking an ewe in a wattled sheep pen, a farmer using a sling to repel crows, the miller busy with his sacks. Mummers would make their rounds at Christmas armed with a stuffed horse's head whose jaws could be moved no doubt with the aim of encouraging generosity in those visited. The Luttrells intermarried with the Paganells, from whom the village takes half its name.

A tithe barn keeps company with the hall and the largely Norman church, All Saints. The old church wears well: ironwork on its south doors is from the early twelfth century. Later that century and during the next, the building was enlarged, but John Loughborough Pearson, when he restored the church in 1875, was no doubt happy to leave *in situ* the eighteenth-century inlaid pulpit. A plaque in the churchyard tells you that the lamps which stand there were installed to mark the diamond jubilee of Queen Victoria and as a mark of 'esteem and affection' for one Mrs Warde-Aldam.

Robin Hood, let it be known once and for all, was as much a Yorkshireman as J.B. Priestley, Captain Cook or Harold Wilson. Or so we insist in Yorkshire. Not only do we find the much-travelled outlaw dealing energetically with pirates at the eponymous Robin Hood's Bay on the North Yorkshire coast: not only are we convinced that he fired his final arrow and breathed his last at Kirklees, near Mirfield; we are also inclined to boast that he married his Maid Marian at Campsall's church of St Mary Magdalene, east of the A1.

Whether the largely Norman church much resembles the one where Robin and Marian took their vows is questionable. Robin, who frequently summoned his merry band by a blast on his horn, was too early to need to hide a smile at the inscription on the fifteenth-century rood screen: *Beware of the devil when he blows his horn*.

Cross the A1, descendant of the old Great North Road, to join the A638 and travel north-westwards to Ackworth, near Pontefract, which contains the resting place of one man and the living memorial to another. The two could hardly be more dissimilar. They were John Gully, one-time MP for Pontefract but far more famous, in his earlier days, as a prizefighter, and Dr John Fothergill, the founder of Ackworth's famous collonaded Quaker school which began life as a foundling hospital in 1758. It became a school, under Dr Fothergill, in 1779.

Four years after that at Wick, near Bristol, John Gully was born. When he was only 13 his father died and John was left to maintain the family single-handed. The burden proved too much for him, and he was imprisoned for debt. But this proved singularly fortunate, for in gaol he met The Game Chicken, otherwise Henry Pearce, a champion boxer, who taught the lad his trade so effectively that Gully became 'the Chicken's' natural successor. After a brilliant career which included a number of successful bouts – one of 36 rounds – against Bob Gregson, 'the Lancashire Giant', Gully turned to gambling, then became a bookie and then – as a result, it is said, of a bet – a Member of Parliament. Twice he successfully stood for Pontefract, but eventually gave up politics because it interfered, he said, with his racing. Ackworth Park, the house he bought for £60 000, reflects his glory no longer (unlike Fothergill's school, which flourishes still), but Gully (for whom Queen Victoria apparently had a tender spot) has his own, rather oblique, memorials in the village. One, in the parish church, St Cuthbert's, records the murder of his son Robert by Chinese after his ship was wrecked off Formosa in 1842. And the other? Beside the churchyard, railed off from the other occupants, John Gully, once champion of England, lies buried in the grave he went to at the age of 94. Another occupant was one of his 24 children (by two wives), a daughter, who was refused Roman Catholic burial in the churchyard by the vicar of the time. Thereupon John, a tough opponent in any dispute, bought a piece of land adjoining the churchyard, railed it off and had it consecrated for his family's use.

At this same village the body of St Cuthbert is said to have rested on the way to its final abiding place in Durham Cathedral. Twice a year in the saint's honour, a sheaf of corn for the birds is tied to the staff held by his little statue above the doorway.

The story of St Cuthbert, if true, demonstrates that there was a church here long before the present, largely nineteenth-century structure arose, and in fact the tower and the south porch are fifteenth-century. Indeed, many ages have contributed to this delightful village: the green has a cross with a medieval shaft topped by a Tudor ball and there are two fine Victorian signposts with striking carved lettering. Pre-dating these is Mary Lowther's Hospital, an almshouse founded in 1741 and still in use. Like the Quaker school, it is evidence of both the poverty and the charity of the eighteenth century.

A vastly different establishment, this, it need hardly be said, from the one Fothergill founded, where at one time the young Quaker pupils, if male, wore cocked hats, tailed coats and leather breeches, and the girls white caps, check aprons and stiff gowns. But any stiffness of discipline was doubtless mellowed by the sense of fun that has so often characterized members of the Friendly Persuasion. Pupils returning to their studies were at one time met at Wentbridge by a cart drawn by the school bull. A fondness for animals seems to have characterized Ackworth, where explorers like David Livingstone and, later, the first great wildlife photographer, Cherry Kearton, were sure of an enthralled audience for their tales of adventure with lions and elephants.

The school bull has been grazing the Elysian fields for a long time now, and no doubt many other animals have enlivened the pupils' days, but the fine range of austere Georgian buildings Fothergill knew stands like a watchdog against any desecration of this elegant village.

To visit Wragby a few miles west of Ackworth on the A638 is to discover yet again the eternal surprise of West Yorkshire. A bare half dozen miles south of Castleford, Henry Moore's birthplace, this may well be one of the rural areas recalled fondly from his childhood.

I approached it through cornfields to find a trim, largely stone-built village with a tiny rectangular green providing a setting for the war memorial. Just down the road is Nostell Priory (famously associated with Chippendale, James Paine and Robert Adam), in the grounds of which stands Wragby's parish church of St Michael and Our Lady. The church has long been famous for the largest collection of Swiss glass in the world, save for that in the Landes Museum in Zurich, which has six hundred panels. Wragby's church had 489 panels or roundels, manufactured between 1514 and 1745. They formerly glorified 17 of the 19 windows in the church, having been put there by the local squire, who brought them back from the Grand Tour in the early 1800s. Sad to tell, they are there no longer, having been moved for safety to York Minster when threatened by subsidence damage due to mining activities under the village.

A Latin inscription on the chancel wall beseeches us to pray for the soul of Prior Alured 'who had this choir built in the ninth year of his Priorate and in the year of our Lord 1533'. Alured was the penultimate prior of St Oswald's, so visitors to the present Nostell Priory (or the magnificent house that now bears the name) might well feel charitable towards him.

The priory ended, as a priory, at the dissolution of the monasteries and its estates were eventually bought by Rowland Winn, a rich London alderman. The family prospered, through selling the coal which the monks had sold before them, and Sir Rowland, the fourth baronet, employed James Paine to design him a new house on the site. On the orders of the fifth baronet (also named Sir Rowland) Robert Adam added a north wing and decorated the interior of the house, now owned by the National Trust. Nostell Priory contains much furniture by Thomas Chippendale, born in Wharfedale at Otley.

At Walton, not far away, lived dear old Charles Waterton, who brought eccentricity to a fine art, though he would protest with sincere bewilderment that he was the least remarkable of men.

The house he lived in, Walton Hall, still stands on its island site, though it is now a hotel. Built in 1765, 17 years before Waterton was born, it occupies the site of a medieval manor house. Here the much-travelled squire created the country's first nature reserve, within whose high surrounding walls every species was protected except the 'Hanoverian' or brown rat, which Waterton, the most patriotic of men, considered a vicious interloper and usurper of the 'true British' black rat.

During his travels he captured an alligator by riding on its back and on another occasion tied up a boa constrictor in his braces. He was so fascinated by the habits of the vampire bat that he would sleep with his big toe protruding from his hammock in the hope of enticing the 'nocturnal surgeon', as he called it, to take a snack. Perhaps this had something to do with his almost fanatical belief in 'tapping the claret' or blood-letting. Most of his exploits took place in South America, but on a visit to Rome his high spirits got the better of him and he climbed to the top of St Peter's and left his gloves on the lightning conductor. This so alarmed the Pope that he appealed for volunteers to remove them, and when none was forthcoming, Waterton demonstrated once more the famed insanity of the English by retrieving them himself.

His life was so consistently strange that it is impossible to encapsulate it in a few lines. He decided on his choice of a bride while he held her in his arms as a baby at her christening, then married her when she was 17 and he 47. Less than a year later, she died in giving birth to the squire's only son: whereupon Waterton became a veritable hermit, living in a sparsely furnished room at the top of the house, rising at 3 a.m. and spending much time in prayer. He was the kindest of men, throwing open the park to visitors, including the inmates of a mental asylum whom he would dance with and row around the lake.

On his 82nd birthday he celebrated by climbing an oak tree, but after a fall in the park, he died. On what would have been his 83rd birthday, his body was borne on a barge to a favourite spot between two well-beloved oaks and here Squire Waterton was laid to rest.

Sandal Magna, with its ruined thirteenth-century castle, now lies within the Wakefield city boundary. Until recently, older residents could still recall the village life that to some extent persists here. A peaceful existence it was before the Kaiser's war, enlivened by visits from the 'dancing' bear which would rise to its hind legs to perform sullen pirouettes at the behest of its seedy owner; or the May Day celebrations, when the ubiquitous horses were decorated with braids and brightly-coloured cockades, their brasses polished to a dazzling brilliance.

Industry was already fully established. At 5.30 in the morning the 'knocker-up' with his long pole would tap at the upstairs windows to summon the workers to their toil at Portobello Mills and 12 hours later their boots could be heard on the homeward road. But for all the hard work, life had still a somehow leisured air, though Sunday brought an almost obligatory day of rest when the tyranny of the mill was

exchanged for regimented religion encased in a framework of attendance, often three times a day, at chapel or the fine, largely fourteenth-
century church, St Helen's.

Basically, the church has changed little since the Battle of Wakefield,
when 2000 Yorkists were killed, making this the biggest Lancastrian
victory of the Wars of the Roses. Richard, Duke of York, left the
shelter of Sandal Castle to lose his life and his head, the latter being sent
by Henry VI's queen, Margaret, to decorate York's Micklegate Bar.

Denby Dale, only a few miles west of Barnsley, is a typical West
Yorkshire blend of the industrial and the agricultural: its mill chimneys
challenge the loftier dominance of the Emley Moor television mast
rising from the climbing land that warns of the moorlands ahead; its
architecture, apart from some interesting old farms, is on the familiar
West Yorkshire pattern. Its chief, perhaps only claim to fame rests on
the villagers' highly idiosyncratic way of celebrating great events: they
make a pie, a gigantic affair, and then invite the rest of the nation to help
them eat it – at so much per portion, of course.

The first pie was possibly the one baked in 1788 to celebrate the
recovery of George III from mental illness. In 1887 they found some
reason for making another pie which went bad and had to be buried
with all decent speed but with appropriate obsequies in Toby Wood:
they say the smell still lingers. Yet even on the funeral card that
announced that pie's demise, a footnote proclaimed THE RESUR-
RECTION PIE! Unlike its predecessor, *this* had been 'made by the ladies of
the village' and was therefore confidently 'expected to be a success'. It
contained 48 stones of flour, 96 stones of potatoes, a heifer, two calves
and two sheep.

The biggest Denby Dale pie to date, made in 1964, required a pie dish
weighing a ton and a half and measuring 18 feet long by six feet wide.
Cocktail parties were held in it as it floated empty on the canal until its
great moment arrived. You might still find, if you search for them,
mementoes in Denby Dale of these triumphs and disasters – plates,
printed cards and the like – but the easiest of all to find is the communal
'Pie Hall', built from the proceeds of that biggest-ever pie.

A few miles to the west and further towards the Pennine heights,
Holmfirth can fairly be said to outdo even Denby Dale in quirkiness
and certainly in the grandeur of its surroundings. Yet these same steep
hills and dizzily descending valleys have often brought disaster when
floods poured into the village.

In the deluge of 1738, caused by a violent thunderstorm, water
forced itself into the parish church during a service, no doubt adding
fervour to some of the prayers. The church was so badly damaged that
it had to be replaced in the eighteenth century by the present building.

In 1821 a reservoir broke its banks as if to warn of the cataclysm that was to befall 31 years later, when the Bilberry Reservoir at the head of the Holme Valley swept away its embankment and poured into the streets taking a toll of 81 lives and causing £250 000 worth of damage. Opposite the church a pillar (nicknamed Old Genn after a former village constable) records the height of the flood, which is also illustrated by a stone set high in the wall of a butcher's shop.

Holmfirth is a stone-built factory village with firm and apparently disparate traditions. Its craftsmanship in the making of fine worsted cloth is recognized the world over. But the men who tend the machines sometimes have other talents. Not for nothing has Holmfirth been called 'a nest of playwrights'. Long before my late friend George Taylor, founder of the Holme Valley Comedy Players, wrote his drama about the Luddites, other dramas and comedies had been enacted by early film-makers, whose slapstick epics often involved large numbers of the villagers, not only as extras but frequently as stars. Sadly, World War I destroyed any hopes of Holmfirth out-doing Hollywood. So James Bamforth, a photographer who had made lantern slides and used real photographs to illustrate Victorian best-sellers, turned his hand to sentimental song cards to send to the boys at the front and, when peace returned, began producing comic seaside postcards which soon made Holmfirth the world's comic card capital.

Holmfirth seems destined for comedy. Surely the ghosts of those silent comedians rejoiced when their old haunts became the setting for *Last of the Summer Wine*, one of the most successful of BBC television comedy shows.

No village in the Holme Valley can hope to escape completely from the pervasive influence of Compo, Foggy and Co. Hence at Hepworth, south of Holmfirth, the Butcher's Arms provides a backcloth now and then for scenes from the series. Not that the villagers are swayed by such fleeting fame. They are probably much prouder of the fact that Hepworth Silver Band attained its centenary in 1982 and only a few years before that not only won the Belle Vue senior cup but produced their own record, stirringly entitled 'Marching with Hepworth'.

Equally patriotic is their choice of signature tune – 'Pratty Flowers March', 'Pratty Flowers' being the title of the venerable 'Holmfirth Anthem', written in the mid-eighteenth century and now often sung when Holme Valley folk foregather.

A familiar sight and sound as they play outside the Butcher's Arms, the band, in their smart uniforms, have their annual hour of glory on the last Monday in June, when Hepworth holds its Feast with a march, hymn-singing and service. Learned opinion suggests that the event has pagan origins, but it is popularly regarded as a thanksgiving for deliverance from the plague which afflicted Hepworth in the sixteenth and seventeenth centuries. Like the pestilence at Eyam in Derbyshire, it was supposedly conveyed from London in a parcel of clothing. As at Eyam, the Hepworth folk stayed put and carried on with their lives, having sealed off the infected part of the village with a barricade near what is now Barracks Fold.

In bygone days, farming and handloom weaving were the chief occupations, but coal mining and the power loom provided more employment. Today, villagers find work sometimes as far afield as Sheffield and Manchester, but no doubt return thankfully at night to the peace of 'the high dwelling', the original meaning of Hepworth.

North of Holmfirth is 'Oodle', officially Wooldale, the sort of name that might have been coined for some fictional village of TV or radio. 'But of course,' some bright-eyed young producer might say, 'what could be better? *Wooldale* – redolent of sheep-shearing and handloom-weaving. Perfect for this sort of bucolic north-country epic!' But the name is too old to allow of so simplistic an explanation and is probably derived from the far less cosy Wolf Dale.

If you wish to see the Holme Valley, get out of Holmfirth and climb to hill-top Wooldale and you feel so near to heaven that it won't surprise you that Wooldale was once a Quaker stronghold missionary base led by an early convert, Henry Jackson, who suffered imprisonment for his heterodoxy. He would be glad to know that the Friends' meeting house in Wooldale still fulfils its original purpose.

George Fox himself visited Wooldale in 1669 during the reign of Charles II. Queen Anne was on the throne when Henry Jackson's son, Elihu, a physician, built Wooldale Hall. Some years older than the hall, the Bay Horse, built in 1691, is now a cottage but the villagers can slake their thirsts at the Lord Nelson. A hundred years ago Wooldale was proud of the high level of attendance at its Board School, which now serves the village as a community centre. In days when few had the leisure for such diversions or the energy after a day's work, most of the community probably supported themselves by weaving and their renovated cottages remain among later dwellings in a variety of styles.

The names of the surrounding villages here seem to breathe antiquity – Upperthong, Netherthong, Honley, Netherton, Thurstonland, Holmbridge, Hade Edge. Each has its story, if we could only tell them all. Almondbury, now overtaken by the sprawl of Huddersfield's expansion, has a notable landmark in the Victoria Tower which provides views of the Colne Valley from the top of Castle Hill, a vantage point to Romans, Brigantes and Normans.

A few miles to the north-west of Holmfirth, in the Colne Valley, lies Marsden. I learned only recently that just as the English make butts of the Irish, and the Americans of the Poles, so apparently do the folk of Huddersfield poke fun at inhabitants of Colne Valley. Or at least, they did in the days when, having to make their own entertainment, folk made it usually at somebody else's expense.

Thus it is said the villagers of Slaithwaite, thinking the reflection of the moon in a canal was really a cheese, tried to rake it out. At Marsden they were more imaginative. Hoping to ensure a perpetual springtime they built a wall round a cuckoo so that its song would echo forever over a balmy and vernal landscape. 'Marsden Cuckoos' the local inhabitants were called by those incapable of appreciating the poetic impulse, or indeed the ingenuity or ambition of the Marsden folk. Was it *their* fault the cuckoo couldn't appreciate its own good luck, and set off in search of something better – in Africa?

The probability is that the so-called Marsden cuckoos, like their cheese-addicted fellow villagers, were simply having a bit of fun at the expense of their rather smug, sober-sided detractors from Huddersfield. After all, what had Huddersfield that Marsden hadn't? Against the far-famed Huddersfield Choral Society, Marsden would confidently pit the Colne Valley Male Voice Choir, and there can be little doubt that they would place Colne Valley cloth on a level with anything produced elsewhere in the environs of 'Smuggersfield', as it was once dubbed by an irreverent journalist.

Marsden is a monument to industrial history. Not only is it the site of such engineering triumphs as the Standedge Tunnels – triple railway tunnels, together with Britain's longest canal tunnel – it enshrines, too, grim memories of the early agonies of industry; of the murder by Luddites of William Horsfall, a Marsden millowner who so loathed the machine-breakers that he would gladly, he said, ride up to his saddle girths in their blood. But it was his own dying blood that dripped from the saddle when Horsfall was ambushed, as he rode home, by four men with pistols.

'Enoch makes them, Enoch shall break them' was the Luddites' rallying cry, in honour of the great hammers with which they smashed the machines they saw as robbers of their livelihood. Both hammers and the hated cropping frames were manufactured by Enoch Taylor, who now lies in a table tomb in a park which was once a Marsden burial ground.

Marsden has the grimness of most South Pennine towns, a characteristic which in no way diminishes the affection they awaken in visitor and resident alike. They sit, like Marsden, surrounded by beauty yet apparently unmoved by it, like a dour great-uncle determined not to enjoy his ninetieth birthday party. In the case of Marsden, the 'golden frame' is provided by majestic moorlands, partly owned by the National Trust, and the lovely Blake Lea and Wessenden Valleys. But Marsden is not quite such a curmudgeon: a Youth Hostel in the town and a small textile museum are proof that it knows the value of its beautiful surroundings and its dramatic and seminal history.

A near neighbour to Marsden is Meltham, locally famed for its Folly Dolly Falls and with the only church to be consecrated (on St Bartholomew's Day 1651) during the period of the Commonwealth following the Civil War. But all these communities have an idiosyncratic charm – Wilshaw, for instance, a lesser known version of the 'model village' Saltaire built by Sir Titus Salt to house his workfolk. But in this case the paternalist nineteenth-century millowner was Joseph Hirst.

Here we are on the fringe of Lancashire – the surely essential Lancashire of Rochdale (Gracie Fields country) and Bury (synonymous with black pudding, though Barnsley in South Yorkshire has a considerable claim to eminence in that culinary field). On either side of the Pennine boundary, giants of industry, Oldham and Huddersfield, challenge the Pennine heights with their factory chimneys, now so often smokeless – a fact which delights the conservationist but breaks the hearts of some old inhabitants of these proud towns.

Some of this territory has long been disputed and will long continue so. Todmorden, for instance, now begrudgingly (if at all) surrendered by Lancashire to Yorkshire, once straddled the county boundary – with what schizophrenic effects on the populace we can only conjecture!

Boulder Clough, above Sowerby Bridge, has an air of discretion appropriate to the birthplace of a secret society, which indeed it claims to be. Its gritstone cottages with their small windows (those at least that have not been 'modernized') seem to look out on the surrounding world of moorland with the watchfulness of old codgers who see all, but – in the time-honoured Yorkshire tradition – say nowt!

The arcane brotherhood known as the Henpecked Club which met here each Whit Monday and still meets at some other ostensibly secret rendezvous is by no means as secretive as it used to be, nor as numerous. Perhaps husbands are less henpecked than they used to be. Or perhaps they never were under serious female domination. As the wife of one member put it, with typical Yorkshire candour and common sense, 'If they were all that henpecked they'd never get away with it.'

Down the hill is Sowerby Bridge, a town that has recently become aware of the tourist potential of South Pennine traditions and won fame and visitors by reviving the rush-bearing ceremonies which in past centuries enlivened village life. The custom began when churches had earthen floors which had to be spread with rushes. Once or twice a year these had to be renewed and in some north-western towns and villages these occasions developed into unique festivals and processions, at the centre of which was the elaborately decorated rush cart drawn by men of the village wearing panama hats and clogs.

South of Sowerby Bridge, a handful of villages, some with old halls built by yeomen clothiers, dot the hilltops. Barkisland has a hall built in 1638 and the Griffin Inn, dating from 1642. Stainland and Holywell Green, too, have corners that exude antiquity. At Greetland, the Spring Rock Inn is a centre for one of Yorkshire's ancient pastimes, knur and spell, otherwise known as nipsy, or poor man's golf, in which the knur, a clay ball, is thrown into the air by a spring called the spell and hit by the players as far as possible with a large-headed springy stick.

Folk in Ripponden still talk about the time when a summer cloudburst swept away part of the parish church, deluging the churchyard and leaving the coffins stranded in the branches of trees. And, Ripponden being the sort of place it is, you might get the impression that the catastrophe occurred a couple of weeks ago instead of in 1722.

Church, bridges and inns in Ripponden are rich in history and legend. The village was a crossroads in Roman and medieval times and where the old bridge now stands there was a Roman ford. The first record of a bridge occurs in 1313. That bridge was probably built of wood, but in 1533, William Firth, of Field House, Sowerby left 7s 6d for the building of a stone bridge.

Ripponden folk are strong-minded and when the then landlord of the Old Bridge Inn, which claims to be the oldest in Yorkshire, fell out with the church folk, he declared that rather than let them use the bridge he would pull it down; it was his anyway, he said, since he'd 'paid a fine of £10'. Without arguing the strange logic of the matter, the then Rector raised £10, gave it to the landlord and declared the matter settled.

Ripponden somehow entwines itself into the history of England. Daniel Defoe stayed at the Old Bridge Inn in the 1720s, then went to Halifax and, quite coincidentally, embarked on the writing of *Robinson Crusoe*. Some years later a writer of a different stamp was busy in Ripponden. He was the incumbent of the time, a Mr Watson, whose *History of Halifax* would be a priceless find today for a fortunate collector.

Half a mile above the road that twists and turns from Halifax to Burnley you will find Luddenden. Before the power-driven mills arose in the valley beside the river, canal and railway, the village was already here, virtually hidden in a cleft in the hills, so tightly fitted, with church and pub and intricately woven lanes and cottages, that you wonder how it was ever built.

Thin and high, these dark gritstone houses stand, with narrow windows that made the most of every last second of daylight, so that the handloom weavers working in the upper storeys could see to guide the shuttle. Yet for all its industrial past, this is a country village, or, rather, a village at the turning point between two cultures, two ages – the cottage industry period of the pre-mechanical age.

For all the complexity of its cobbled streets there is a dignified unity in the neat square with its war memorial – impressive for such a tiny place – in front of the church. The Lord Nelson Inn was packed with invading motor-cyclists on my last visit. Would Branwell Brontë have enjoyed this robust company if he had dropped in as he often did when he was ticket collector for two years at Luddenden Foot railway station? He came not only to drink but, surprisingly, to borrow books at a subscription of 4d a month from a theological library bequeathed to the inn by a departed vicar, when that worthy perhaps made his last journey across the bridge over the beck, to rest in the graveyard of his church. There, too, lies Thomas Murgatroyd, the wool man who lived in Kershaw House, a 1650 mansion befitting his status as the owner of the mill across the valley.

The inn began life as a private house, rebuilt in 1634 by a churchwarden, Gregory Patchett. In 1745, when it became an inn, the clergy seem to have treated it almost as an annexe to the church and regaled visiting preachers with food and wine here. At first it was called The Black Swan; its name was changed to the Lord Nelson after Trafalgar in honour of England's hero, whose image adorns the inn sign. A less illustrious memorial is the pair of lock-ups in the wall of the school, labelled respectively MIDGLEY and WARLEY, a relic of the time when the boundary of the parishes ran through the middle of the school – it would never have done, apparently, for one parish to have housed a miscreant from another.

A mile or two to the west, Midgley is renowned for its Pace Egg Play, performed nowadays by boys of Calder High School, Mytholmroyd, on Good Friday in the towns and villages of the area, including Luddenden itself. This somewhat eccentric drama is based on the Easter version of the old Mumming Play, and with all its strange characters in their even stranger attire, affords huge enjoyment to both performers and audience.

When I last saw it, the active rôles were still performed exclusively by boys, the girls apparently content to be collectors for whatever charity was to benefit. It is difficult, in these days, to believe that the boys will be allowed to maintain their monopoly much longer, though the cast is 'macho' in the extreme – St George, Slasher, the Doctor, the Black Morocco Prince and Tosspot 'fume and strut' their usually boastful way across the streetside 'stages', more often than not wielding their wooden swords in what appears to be mortal combat, until the defeated one is revived by the Doctor, who boasts of having 'travelled in doctorship'

> *From Italy, Titaly, High Germany, France and Spain,*
> *And now I'm returned to cure disease in Old England again.*

He can cure

> *The itch, the stitch, the palsy and the gout*
> *If a man has 19 devils in his soul,*
> *I can cast 20 of them out.*
> *I have in my pocket crutches for lame ducks*
> *Spectacles for blind hummer bees and pack-saddles for broken-backed mice.*
> *I cured Sir Harry of a nang nail almost 55 yards long*
> *So surely I can cure this poor man.*

And cure him, of course, he can.

The last character to appear is Old Toss Pot

> *He's a gallant old man*
> *An' he wears a degree.*
> *He's a stick in his hand*
> *An' he wears a pig tail*
> *An' he takes his delight*
> *In drinking mulled ale.*

Toss Pot sings:

> *I've some eggs in my basket although I appear*
> *Eggerpecting [expecting] sometime to come in for my share.*
> *Although I am ragged*
> *And not so well dressed*
> *I can kiss some bonny lasses*
> *As well as the best.*

While the other players sing the traditional Pace Egg song in which they beg for money, 'sweet eggs and strong beer', as once their forebears begged at houses and farms throughout the district, Toss Pot collects coppers for charity.

With their traditional smocks adorned with enormous rosettes, their hats trimmed with paper flowers, their traditional props – swords, bugle, tambourines and the Doctor's bag of infallible remedies – the players awake in their audience an enjoyment that matches their own enormous gusto. Here, if anywhere, is a village tradition that not only survives but thrives. Nor is it a revival from the distant past. As recently as 1977 the late Mr Harry Greenwood recalled in his book *Memories* that as boys, he and his friends would tour the district on Good Friday with their play and collect perhaps five shillings each which they would spend at Todmorden Fair. Two months before the next Good Friday, preparations, rehearsals and costume-making for the next play began to provide something to do in the cold, dark days of early spring.

Heptonstall is the classic South Pennine village, reached by climbing a steep hill from Hebden Bridge. Its haunted air is bolstered by the presence, beside the present church, of a ruin whose tower lost its west front in a great storm of 1847, a fate perhaps seen by John Wesley as an act of divine retribution. He had preached in it five times and so maybe felt qualified to condemn it as 'the ugliest church I know'. He presumably fancied himself in the realm of church architecture, since the village contains an octagonal chapel built to his own design, which claims now to be the oldest Methodist chapel in the world still in continuous use.

But Wesley was not the haunting sort. When the trumpet called he had presumably no wish to hang about in the company of such shades as the counterfeiter David Hartley, unless he felt 'King David' had a soul to save. The coiner king could have repented, I suppose, when the York prison chaplain read the burial service before him as he stood on the infamous 'drop of York'. But be that as it may, there was little forgiveness for Hartley in Heptonstall, when they brought his broken-necked corpse home for burial, and – shamefacedly, in Latin – recorded the event in church records:

1770 May 1st. David Hartley, of Bell House in the township of Erringden hanged by the neck near York for unlawfully stamping and clipping a public coin.

The latest occupant of Bell House is still, for all I know, a full-bearded poet, Gordon Hoyles, who ekes out a living by dry stone walling between inscribing his poems on such unusual surfaces as the sides of old gas ovens. His life resembles Hartley's in its primitive conditions, but surely in nothing else; for Hoyles has a fine contempt for money, whereas Hartley's illegal efforts to make the gold coinage of his day proliferate cost him his life.

David lies in his consecrated patch of earth (located by counting 12 stone slabs in a straight line from the porch of the old church, then two spaces down to the left) and, since death makes strange bedfellows, he shares his resting place with medieval priests, who may or may not dispute with and rebuke him when the night winds of winter try to emulate the 'great storm' which brought the west tower wall crashing down over a century ago.

Weary of their moralising, David may look through the windows of the Old Grammar School where boys no longer carve their names on the black oak desks. The school was endowed in 1642, then in 1829 its scholastic career ended and it became a branch of the Yorkshire Penny Bank. With refreshing wisdom, the bank kept the old place unchanged, relinquishing it to the local authority in 1954. Now it is a museum.

The old Victorian furnishings of the church have been swept away to make room for a light and airy open-plan interior; the old cloth hall, known by the handloom weavers, remains in its outward form, though now in use as cottages. Nearby is Weavers' Square, where change is more obvious: once it was the site of handloom weavers' cottages, but today it serves as a possibly unique museum of stone, incorporating granite setts, pebbles, cobbles and old floor flags.

Once a charnel house piled high with skeletons, Chantry House has gravestones and coffin lids built into its structure. Bones still crop up from time to time and at least one ghost is on record: it appeared at a long forgotten doorway during renovations – and, some say, beckoned. Whether any further work was done that day is not recorded ...

Once a year, about the end of June, all these ghosts must stand amazed, as the grey stones form a dour backcloth for vivid figures in the costume of other times or maybe other lands, depending on the theme of Heptonstall's summer festival.

I would rather visit Heptonstall in the quiet dusk of a summer evening. As you walk along narrow Northgate, passing Wesley's old chapel, the stone setts eventually give way to a rough path; there seems to be an outsize cat on every window sill. Stone-framed entrances sometimes bearing initials and long-past dates, allow glimpses of courts and yards. Across the valley, the hilltop brings home to you how high this superb village hangs in the air.

Not long ago a self-professed witch wanted to buy the then disused Heptonstall Slack Baptist Chapel for use by a witches' coven. The local press made much play with her reported talk of 'projections' and 'forces' ringing the chapel, but the village folk were less alarmed than incredulous, and a retired Baptist minister, Percy Nuttall, horrified by the thought that the old place of Christian worship might witness 'pagan rites', bought the building to transform it into an 'outward bound' and community centre. So far as I know, no magical events have occurred to disturb the peace of Heptonstall.

Can a village be haunted by its past? For all the talk of latter-day witches, this hill top village's sombre aspect is due more to its millstone grit construction than to its history. And yet its story has a gloomy ring. In 1631 the great plague breathed icily upon its people. Only a dozen years after, during the Civil War, the Parliamentarians held it as a garrison and the foolhardy Royalists, incensed by the impunity of its raiding parties, paid dearly when they came by night to take it. The Roundheads rolled boulders down the hillside on the advancing troops and the River Calder, then in spate, joined in against the King's men, many of whom perished in its waters.

A mile or so south of Todmorden lie Mankinholes and Lumbutts, to reach which you must cross the canal by narrow stone bridges, then climb ... The road is narrow and twisting, but the effort is well worth while, whether you use your legs or wheels. Mankinholes is straight out of the packhorse era, even equipped with stone water troughs for the pack trains that pass this way only as ghosts or memories now. Many of the houses are pure seventeenth century. From the Top Brink Inn at Lumbutts you look down on stone-slated cottages deep in the valley to which the ground falls away so suddenly that you see the aptness of the pub's name. On the skyline behind rises Stoodley Pike, the 120-foot monument raised in 1815 to celebrate the end of the Napoleonic Wars.

Much nearer at hand, an angular stone tower rises almost like a Scottish laird's castle in the highlands. But this is no castle, despite the broken parapet of fretted stone that fringes its roof. It was built to house a water wheel, and beside it rushes a fast, noisy stream almost hidden by ferns. Its source, Lee Dam, is a quiet moorland pool for most of the time, yet on the Sunday nearest to New Year's Day – be it snowing, blowing or frozen hard, it offers an amazing spectacle – the New Year Swim.

The custom began when Todmorden decided to raise money for the provision of swimming baths. But today, long after the building of the baths, the swim continues, nowadays ostensibly to raise money for Todmorden Carnival. Even in summer the steel-grey pool surrounded by scrubby trees amid the bare Pennine moors offers little for our comfort, but in the early January days it truly offers naught ... except an icy challenge only humans are brave enough or rash enough to accept.

A little to the east of Mankinholes is Cragg Vale, 'the Coiners' Valley', where counterfeiters pursued the 'Yellow Trade' of clipping gold coins to enrich themselves by making new ones. Their leader, 'King David' (David Hartley) lies, as we saw, in the churchyard at Heptonstall. The coiners' activities led to murder in 1769 when an excise man was sent to track them down. Some of the equipment used by the coiners can be seen at the Hinchliffe Arms in Cragg village.

To the north of Halifax lies what is cosily called Brontëland, though there is little that's cosy about this land of moorland villages, becks and reservoirs flanked to the east and west by industrial Lancashire and West Yorkshire.

My friend, Peggy Hewitt, who has lived here all her life, conveys the district's haunting quality in her book *These Lonely Mountains*. The title is a quotation from Emily Brontë's lines

> *What have these lonely mountains worth revealing?*
> *More glory and more grief than I can tell:*
> *The earth that wakes one human heart to feeling*
> *Can centre both the worlds of Heaven and Hell.*

The Brontë moors are mountains in essence only, writes Peggy Hewitt, 'yet they have all the grandeur and mystical qualities of much loftier places...

'In any weather the moors are beautiful. When the mist swirls and eddies in the valleys, the crests of the hills sail like a fleet of ships on a silent grey sea; as it creeps up to engulf even these, the outlines of the old farms are like faint monotone photographs of long ago. And through the mist, in soft echoes, drift the hopes, the passions and the fears of folk who have lived and worked and died there. Many of these farms are empty now, their floors deep in the dung of the moorland sheep, and old discoloured wallpaper, once carefully chosen, hangs in pathetic ribbons from the walls like whisps of hair clinging to a skull. The stone hearths are cold and bare, where children sat and wriggled their toes out of clogs to warm them at the blaze, and the wind whips the mist as it creeps through sockets of doors and windows.

'Summer is a passing thing, least remembered, gone like a dream, abdicating in royal robes of heather to golden autumn and the turning bracken. The moors spread beneath an infinite blue sky and by the streams the little valleys are generous with blackberries and the orange fruit of rowan and wild rose. Purple shadows fill the gullies in the evening and the plaintive cry of the curlew hangs in the still air.'

Historically, as well as geographically, Thornton is a good starting place for a tour of the Brontë villages. When Patrick Brontë came here as a young clergyman in 1815, Thornton was no more than a small hamlet built of grey stone from quarries nearby. The house to which he brought his wife Maria and their two young children, 74 Market Street, is today marked with a plaque on the wall which announces that within were born four members of the Brontë family – Charlotte in 1816; Branwell the following year, Emily in 1818 and Anne, who arrived in 1820.

This stone-built village of quaint cottages, old hall and ruined church had been a hotbed of puritanism in former days, and when Patrick arrived was still vigorously Nonconformist. Unless his Methodist sympathies were still unawakened, that fact would cause him little distress. Kipping Chapel, built in 1769, was then a focus of white-hot evangelical zeal: today it stands empty. But the sixteenth-century Thornton Hall is still here, with its stone-mullioned windows, ivy-clad porch and old stocks in the driveway.

St James's Church contains the seventeenth-century font where all the Brontë children except Maria were christened. It was doubtless taken there from the Old Bell Chapel where Patrick preached for the first five years of his ministry in the village. Now all that remains is the crumbling east wall and the lonely bell tower Patrick built into the chapel when he had the south-side rebuilt and a new roof made.

Only three miles from Bradford, Thornton is strangely overlooked by many of the Brontë-worshippers who flock to Haworth, six miles away, in their thousands. In its old, isolated days the most convenient form of 'public transport' was a milk cart which left the old Pack Horse Yard, Bradford, three or four times a week. The fare was an exorbitant fourpence a passenger.

From Thornton we journey (as did Patrick and Maria with their children and possessions loaded into seven horse-drawn carts) through Denholme, over the moors to Oxenhope, then into the Worth Valley and up Haworth's steep, stone-setted main street, now barred to wheeled traffic.

Haworth is without doubt the most famous village in Yorkshire. As an English literary shrine it is second only to Stratford-on-Avon. Every year, thousands who have never read a word the Brontës wrote visit Haworth. There are other thousands, of course, who know the Brontës almost as intimately as they know their friends; who feel the influence of Parson Patrick's brood of geniuses as almost tangible presences in the plain, almost forbidding Parsonage, now a museum maintained by the Brontë Society.

Such devotees have visited Haworth since the Brontës themselves lived and died here. Other visitors, some of whom do not consider it worthwhile even to enter the museum, are carried here by coaches as part of enterprising Bradford's policy of attracting tourists to make up some of the losses suffered by the once-dominant wool trade. From Surrey or Kent or elsewhere in the strange world 'down south' they come to marvel at the breathtakingly steep hills, stone-setted and dark, and the small, irregular fields, and try to interpret the uncouth language of the folk to whom these narrow streets lined with glowering houses are as much a home as they were to Charlotte, Emily, Anne and Branwell.

Haworth, if the most famous, is also one of the ugliest of Yorkshire villages. And unless the judges were Brontë addicts, it would surely fare even better in a contest to find the most depressing. Even in the days when Charlotte could describe it as 'the little wild moorland village', it had a grim and gloomy air not unconnected with the churchyard at the top of the steep street. Nor was the churchyard gloomy merely in aspect. Parson Patrick said it was a source of disease and death.

The old Haworth the Brontës knew is still there, or most of it, though the church was replaced by Patrick's successor, the Rev. J. W. Wade, in 1880.

Even in those early days of the Brontë cult, he was criticized for vandalism. In recent years that cult has taken a different turn as poets, novelists and biographers, but particularly novelists, have become increasingly fascinated by the characters who peopled the Haworth scene at the time of the Evangelical Revival and the Industrial Revolution. One such, William Grimshaw, who preceded Patrick as curate-in-charge, has won enduring fame for horse-whipping drunkards to church while the congregation was occupied in singing a particularly long hymn. Whether his oddities were rooted in the kind of sexual repression so beloved of present-day detractors and amateur analysts will perhaps never be known.

Both John and Charles Wesley, founders of the Methodist movement, were great friends of the redoubtable Grimshaw and often preached at Haworth. An entry in John Wesley's *Journal* records a typical visit: '1761: 12 July – I had appointed to be at Haworth, but the church would not near contain the people who came from all sides; however Mr Grimshaw had provided for this by fixing a scaffold on the outside of one of the windows, through which I went after prayers, and the people likewise all went out into the churchyard. The afternoon congregation was larger still. What has God wrought in the midst of these rough mountains?'

The Wesleys may have been the Billy Grahams of their day and certain to draw the crowds, but Grimshaw could manage well enough without their aid. So great was the number of worshippers that flocked to his services that two enormous pewter flagons (still cherished by the church at Haworth) were needed to hold the wine for sometimes as many as 1500 communicants.

Also prized is an ancient silver chalice which long ago became too fragile for general use, and parish registers dating from 1645 record not only the minutiae of village life but events of such weighty national import as the execution of Charles I, the Restoration of the Monarchy and the Plague in London. What we are to make of the apparent appearance of *three* suns in the sky one day will probably never be explained. An early UFO sighting, perhaps? No doubt the evangelical Mr Grimshaw would have found a suitably apocalyptic interpretation for the marvel. Or perhaps the witness had simply spent too long in the Black Bull.

Certainly in later years poor Branwell found that hostelry almost impossible to avoid, though he was no doubt willing enough when the landlord sent for him to entertain guests from out of town with his educated conversation.

On the day Patrick and Maria arrived here in 1820 they could have had no inkling of the tragic days that lay ahead. Maria died in 1825, the same year that carried off Elizabeth. Branwell, Emily and Anne each survived for about 30 years, while Charlotte, the only one to marry, died of consumption when she was 38 and in the early stages of pregnancy. Her tragic cry surely epitomizes the Brontë theme. 'I am not going to die, am I?' she asked her husband, Arthur Nicholls, her father's curate. 'He will not separate us, we who have been so happy.'

Yet life was not all gloom. Emily, at least, delighted in her moorland surroundings and the places that the Brontë children loved may be visited today. For instance, the Brontë Waterfall (no Niagara) and the Brontë Bridge, destination, it is said, for a favourite walk of the sisters.

It is easy to forget that there was a Haworth before ever the Brontës arrived here. Certainly there was a church there long before 1300, though a Latin inscription on a stone by the west wall, referring to a monastery existing in Haworth in the year 600, is believed to be a mistranslation of an earlier inscription.

But few visitors today are interested in any inscriptions but those concerning the Brontës, and chief among these is the one marking the crypt where all the Brontës except Anne, who died of tuberculosis at Scarborough, are buried. In the Brontë Memorial Chapel there used to be a monument to the entire Brontë family carved by John Brown, the church sexton, who was Branwell's devoted friend and whose hand Branwell seized a few minutes before he died in his father's arms.

Buried in the churchyard are other faithful friends and servants of the family. Near a vanished gateway, once used only for Brontë family funerals, lie Martha Brown and Tabitha Ackroyd in the shade of the Parsonage garden wall.

Few churchyards have been more photographed than Haworth's, where from some angles, the serried ranks of tombstones appear to be marching inexorably upon the parsonage. What effect this had upon the Brontë children it is impossible to say. Death was probably too commonplace an event to hold any Gothick horrors for them. In 1850 the average age at death in the village was 28.5, so perhaps we distort the facts with our twentieth-century viewpoint when we speak of their 'tragically early deaths'. Patrick, who died in his 85th year, must have seemed an ancient indeed and his 41-year tenure of the pulpit at Haworth a comparative eternity.

Eternity, indeed, was as much a fact to the Brontës with their deep religious faith, as death itself. Life may have appeared to give them little, apart from the sisters' hard-won fame, but what mattered far more than this life to the devout was their fate in the life beyond. Even so, though earnest they undoubtedly were, including even the wayward Branwell in his soberer moments, their childhood was far from miserable. In the miniature world they created and chronicled in minutely written books to be seen now in the Parsonage Museum, they found a wonderful happiness.

And surely the children would have thrilled to another phenomenon that has brought fame and crowds to Haworth, though these visitors are of almost a different species to the literary scholars or sentimental pilgrims who pore over the manuscripts and drawings or grow misty-eyed at the sight of Emily's comb.

These other visitors find their reading matter in the bookstall at Haworth Station, which abounds in volumes bristling with the technicalities of pistons and boilers, funnels and tenders. For Haworth is the home of the Keighley and Worth Valley Railway, which never operated during the lifetime of the Brontës, though if Patrick had lived a few more years he might have been present in 1867 at the opening of the five-mile line to connect Keighley with the villages of Oakworth, Haworth and Oxenhope. For nearly a hundred years the steam trains puffed untiringly about their business; then in 1962 the line was declared uneconomic, and closed. It was reopened in 1968 by a group of volunteers calling themselves the Keighley and Worth Valley Railway Society and dedicated to the loving preservation of whatever can be preserved of the Age of Steam. At the society's headquarters at Haworth Station, these volunteers chip rust from ancient locomotives gathered from many sources and perform painstaking feats of restoration to add these veterans to the K and WVR stable.

Every weekend from March to October, the Worth Valley echoes again to the sound of steam travel as trains leave Keighley station, shared with British Rail, to climb the five miles to Oxenhope, where the society has a railway museum. On the journey, which includes a climb of 330 feet up an average gradient of 1 in 76, the line goes by way of Ingrow, Damems (once the smallest full-size station in England), Oakworth and Haworth.

The star of the line is generally considered to be Oakworth, which must surely be as conceited as any railway station can become – if it is not rather bored by now at being endlessly described as the station used in the filming of *The Railway Children* (based on E. Nesbit's book) and other TV and screen epics. As if that were not enough, Oakworth has been judged 'Best Preserved Station in Britain'. (No wonder Queen Victoria's portrait seemed to exude stern approval as she looked down from the wall of the stationmaster's office on its youthful occupant, a volunteer like the rest of the staff, despite his smartly professional uniform.)

But Victoria's realm extends beyond the station. Oakworth's Holden Park is a concrete fantasy, with rockery, grottoes, mysterious caverns and an artificial tree trunk which hides a stairway within its convoluted form. Here, in a house long ago vanished and now replaced by a bowling green, lived Sir Isaac Holden, a Victorian of the Victorians.

Born in 1807, the son of a Glasgow coal miner, he started work in the local mills, graduating to teaching, which profession took him to Reading Academy, where he stumbled – almost literally – on his great invention. Rising at 4 a.m. to study, he had to fumble with flint and tinder to provide a light and felt characteristically frustrated by such a waste of time and energy. Thereupon, Isaac promptly invented the Lucifer safety match. He could easily have made a fortune from that alone had he not felt it would be immoral to profit from the almost accidental fruit of 'a happy thought'. Others, less inhibited, were glad to fill his conscientious gap.

Not that Isaac, as a true Methodist of the time, was slothful in business. He knew how to drive a bargain, though the one he struck with a Cullingworth (near Keighley) firm of worsted manufacturers, Townend Brothers, probably left the other party rubbing his hands under the impression that he was the winner.

'I will come and be your book-keeper', said Isaac, 'on condition you allow me two hours' exercise per day in the fresh air – from 7 to 8 a.m. and from 11 to noon,' the hours of exercise to be taken in lieu of annual holidays. In no time at all Isaac was made mill manager and then a partner in the firm. When he handed in his notice, since the Townend Brothers could no longer keep up with him – what with improving the wool combing machinery and introducing a new yarn – he graciously agreed to stay on for a year until his place had been filled by not one man, but *three*, trained for that exacting post.

If you hate Victoriana you may well think that amid all Holden's benefactions to health and education, his periods of vegetarianism, his patronage of the arts, his philosophising on health, backed up by masochistic walks to work in the snow when he was over 80, his creation of Holden Park was his only crime.

The train puffs on . . .

Next stop, Haworth, with its refreshments, bookshop and loco works, then to Oxenhope, whose inhabitants tend to see Haworth as something of an upstart which has overshadowed them for years. Oxenhope was once a thriving grain-growing area, they say. Some of its upland farms were cleared when major waterworks for Bradford arrived. With industrialization, its character changed again. Five big mills once provided steady work but with the general shrinkage of the textile trade many of the inhabitants had to seek work elsewhere.

Oxenhope, for all the grumbling of its residents, inspires the kind of devotion only a village can. It has a Village Society to protect its community interests and to make sure that Big Brother Bradford knows what it thinks. And it stages its annual Straw Race in aid of the local Sue Ryder Home, situated in a former mill owner's house.

A Straw Race? Here again is proof, were it needed, of the unfailing originality and good humour of village life. Not for Oxenhope such hackneyed diversions as bed races or pram races. When they decided to hold an annual charity event, it had to be something they would never dream of holding in, say, Haworth, or even Oakworth. Hence the Straw Race.

On a three-mile course from the Waggon and Horses Inn on the Hebden Bridge Road, the contestants run in pairs to the Bay Horse Inn, where they pick up a bale of straw and carry it to various hostelries, drinking between them a pint of ale at each pub except the last, the Dog and Gun. No new-fangled ideas about sexual equality have apparently reached Oxenhope, for women's teams carry only half a bale and so, quite logically, need only drink half a pint at each pub. For the statistically minded, the organizers offer the information that the 620 contestants run a total of 1800 miles and drink 200 gallons of beer while carrying a total of four tons of straw.

Nearly five years after the Brontës' arrival at Haworth, on 25 July 1825, Patrick baptised Timothy Feather. That was probably the last occasion in his life on which young Master Feather would be called anything but Timmy. As the last of the Pennine handloom weavers he was to achieve a fame that never approached that of the Brontës themselves, but would have astonished them and him.

At one time these Pennine hills were populated by a race of cottagers whose looms rattled all day and long into the night to produce fine cloth on a loom which, in Timmy's case, shared the upper room with his bed and sack of hen food.

He was a popular, colourful, even romantic figure whose life seemed to epitomize much of the history and flavour of the old moorland way of life. Less than five feet tall, he once won a jumping contest for his native village, Stanbury, against Haworth, little more than a mile away. In his youth he had been a famous clog dancer. Small he may have been, but in his later years, a white beard and a halo of white hair added a distinction to his simple dignity.

A life-long bachelor, he had loved Tilda who lived at a farm nearby, and as proof of his affection, sent her a specially woven cotton love-piece. Tilda, alas, was unimpressed. 'Tak' it back,' she told the child who had taken her Timmy's token. 'Ah doan't want it.' And Timmy, so far as we know, never loved another.

The Industrial Revolution meant the end of the handloom cottage industry. As proof that ''ard work niver killed onnybody', Timmy lived until 1910, when he was well into his eighties. Before then he had indeed become a legend, an achievement he would have been very happy to avoid. He got 'stalled' (weary), he said, 'o' foak comin' an' starin' rahnd'.

Stanbury is easy to find. Signposts in Haworth direct you westward to this cluster of cottages in the bottom of the Worth Valley. Here, in the parish church, is the three-decker pulpit (now reduced to two) once used by Patrick at Haworth. A little further along you reach the Old Silent Inn and then pass Ponden Reservoir, which figures in someone's novel as Sorrowful Water. Old Timmy Feather's cottage used to overlook this lonely lake and the surrounding moors. Near here stand Ponden Hall and Ponden Kirk, south of which is Top Withens, a ruined Elizabethan farmhouse, probably the original of Wuthering Heights in Emily Brontë's great book.

Just beyond Stanbury is a hamlet called Scar Top, whose gaunt stone chapel reflects the impregnable spiritual independence of the people who in 1818 built the first Scar Top Chapel (demolished and rebuilt after a storm in 1869) in their spare time. Scar Top was famous for its 'Charity', to which thousands came to sing, listen to sermons – and, when the opportunity arose, to 'cop on', that is, to find a companion of the opposite sex.

In 1880, quarry workers employed just outside the village of Lothersdale, where we begin our tour of Airedale, discovered bones which proved that this homely hamlet had once been the haunt of such exotica as the slender-nosed rhino, the hyena, the straight-tusked elephant and even the lordly lion – none of which out-of-the-way Lothersdale had ever seen within living memory, even in a travelling menagerie.

A retiring place, Lothersdale, whose seclusion offered a haven of peace to Quakers during a period of persecution in Charles II's days. More recently, Charlotte Brontë worked here as governess to the children of John Benson Sidgwick: a man of distinction he must have been in Lothersdale since he had the Archbishop of Canterbury, Edward White Benson, no less, for a cousin. Sidgwick lived at a house called Stone Gappe which Charlotte is said to have used as a model for Gateshead Hall in *Jane Eyre*. The house is reputed to have served as the first Youth Hostel in Yorkshire before it reverted to private ownership. Charlotte would have been less surprised than we are by another of Lothersdale's treasures, the biggest water wheel in England, still to be found in the mill there.

The village notice board epitomizes rural life, advertising (or it did on my last visit) a vacancy for an 'almsperson' for the Spencer Homes Charity, an Open Day at a local kennels and an appeal for cricketers for a village team.

Bethel Methodist Chapel, built in 1851 on 'ground given by the Earl of Burlington', was all set to celebrate Wesley Day with a rousing singing session. A man cutting the grass in the burial ground invited me to take a look inside the chapel, now neatly converted into a two-floor building. He was proud as all Lothersdale folk are proud, of the ancient village with its charming place-names like Rose in the Dale.

The Parish Council has placed a plaque to mark the site of the old pinfold and about ten years ago produced a handsome, hard-backed volume recording *The History of Lothersdale*. Let us hope that such villages have not only a past, but a future.

From Marsden and Meltham, with occasional diversions, our route has roughly followed the Pennine Way. And it does so still – at some peril – for at Thornton in Craven we are a mere broomstick flight from witch-haunted Pendle Hill in Lancashire. Thornton is as self-effacing as Lothersdale, yet two writers at least have found something to say about it.

One was the indefatigable Arthur Mee, in whose book *The West Riding* Thornton receives its meed of praise for four things – the lovely views afforded by its situation on the hillside above the Earby Beck, its almshouses dating from the year of Waterloo, its green, complete with stocks, and its 'lowly little church'.

The inscription on the almshouses is plain enough. They were endowed for five poor women 'pursuant to the desire of Joseph Smith late of the City of London, banker, a native of this parish', and very pleasant – if small – dwellings they must have proved for the women who have lived in them down the years since Waterloo.

If Arthur Mee managed a respectful paragraph or two on Thornton, Roger Mason wrote a whole book – *Granny's Village*; the Granny being his own, who occupied Love Tree Cottage, which still stands next to the Post Office.

The village has changed little since his Granny was born in 1882. Photographs of her appear throughout the book at various stages of her life – in a group picture of schoolchildren when she was seven, solicitously holding her little brother Reuben's hand; and, at 94, patient of face and nearly sightless, not at all fussed to be photographed for grandson Roger's book.

Perhaps in imagination she was recalling the Thornton characters she had known during her long life in 'her' village – the farmers, craftsmen, millowners and quarrymen, and her own father whose dusty workshop had remained unchanged (a magical place for young Roger) since the old man downed tools for ever.

Thornton indeed has changed little. A map of the village as it was at the turn of the century shows manor house, rectory, school, green, the Love Tree and Cowgill Farm straggling along the top stroke of the T made by Earby Road, Old Road and Station Road.

Follow the Pennine Way now to Gargrave, and if you value quietude, go there in winter, when it is difficult to imagine that the village's peace was ever disturbed – other than by one Abe Beecroft caught 'imbibing during divine service' and sentenced to the stocks which once stood near St Andrew's Church. Abe was the last offender to suffer here in that fashion, as he was also the last occupier of squatter's cottage on the middle green.

That was before the nineteenth century, which was indeed a time of upheaval for this Craven village straddling the River Aire. Who would

think today that the Luddite rioters would strike here (just as they did
in industrial Huddersfield and Halifax) destroying the new power
looms which, surprisingly, once stood in Mason's mill, again on the
middle green.

Such turbulent days are past, it seems, and Gargrave is the scene in
summer of the much happier activity of canal holidaymakers
rediscovering their land-legs by venturing ashore to the Anchor Inn,
which used to offer the most unexpected attractions of a miniature
Whipsnade.

Or they may venture along the High Green to the Singing Kettle, or
drop in at the Mason's Arms or the Swan Inn. They can be confident
that Gargrave will welcome them: it has long been used to visitors on
their way to somewhere, for it rests in the Aire Gap which has afforded
passage through the Pennine hills to Roman and Viking, monk and
merchant.

At an ancient ford, a Roman once cast a coin bearing the image of the
Emperor Domitian into the Aire in spate, to appease whatever gods he
revered, and during the last war, schoolboy diggers for victory
unearthed other coins, this time showing the head of Edward III.

In 1120 this village had a saint, no less, as a priest – St Robert of
Newminster, as he became. It was another saint – Andrew – who by
reason of his patronage, saved the parish church in about 1314 from
being destroyed by raiding Scots. Since six churches had already been
razed here it might seem that diplomacy had proved the better part of
piety.

From Gargrave the Pennine Way leads into Malhamdale, marvellously rewarding, for within a small area at the head of the dale are
Malham Tarn, a lake on top of a mountain, as someone recently called
it; Malham Cove, with its crescent cliffs 300 feet high in places, and
Gordale Scar, a great 'roofless cave' and – like Malham Cove – a
consequence of the mid-Craven fault.

But first we must travel up dale by way of Bell Busk, then Airton,
with its early Quaker meeting house keeping company with 300-year-
old houses around the green and the old riverside mill, now a delightful
home for flat-dwellers. Up the hill is Calton, where Oliver Cromwell
stayed at the Hall with Colonel John Lambert. A man in the Fairfax
mould of great Parliamentarians, Lambert must often have sighed for
Calton during his exile in Guernsey imposed by a vengeful Charles II.

At Hanlith, a little to the west of the main road, there is a delightful
picnic area, but don't linger there so long that you have no time to
explore Hanlith's near neighbour, Kirkby Malham. This village is for
me the queen of the dale. You may walk here by one riverside path
from Hanlith and return by another, and if all you see is the church,
your journey will still have been worthwhile. Its long, low structure

contains monuments to the Lamberts, revered by the locals if not by King Charles, while the panelling in the chancel commemorates Walter Morrison, friend of Kingsley and Darwin, and local benefactor who lived at Malham Tarn House.

It was the bells of St Michael the Archangel that Tom the chimney-sweep (in Kingsley's *The Water Babies*) heard as he came down the river. No wonder Kingsley found this part of the Dales so enchanting. And enchanting it remains, despite the multitudes of tourists lured this way by Malham.

Near St Michael's Church at Kirkby Malham there stands the Victoria Hotel and, conveniently close to the pub, the old stocks. But now even scolds and witches may come here with confidence, for the old ducking stool which stood here has vanished.

Malham itself, near the head of this dale, is as essential to Yorkshire as Scarborough, Harrogate or Ilkley Moor, an ancient place as its halls and houses prove. Here the monks of Fountains Abbey had the equivalent of a medieval estate office to deal with their considerable business in moor-run sheep. Not far away, at Bordley, east of Gordale Scar, they bred horses, too, that were renowned beyond the dales.

Malham today, the destination of Youth Hostellers and Pennine Way walkers, sees perhaps fewer sheep than people – at least in summer. They crowd its excellent information centre and wander among the eighteenth-century houses, mostly built of limestone, the same weather-worn silvery stuff which forms Malham Cove, from the foot of which emerges Malham Beck to run through the centre of the village. But unless they climb to the top of the Cove they will miss the magnificent view from the fantastic limestone pavement of the valley with its Celtic fields.

2

Ribblesdale to Dentdale

ELGAR'S DOG AND ADAM SEDGWICK

Nappa, by the east bank of the Ribble, calls itself 'the last hamlet in Yorkshire'. It might just as accurately claim to be the first – and one of the smallest. At a recent count, 16 people were living in its four houses, one of which served also as the pub. Ask Nappa folk about their hamlet's history and they might scratch their heads and then remember that there was a cockfight here in 1885...

Compared with Nappa, Long Preston, a few miles up-dale, is almost a city. It is surely well-named, for its main street seems reluctant to peter out among the fields and fells. And yet its straggling progress is full of interest, with pubs and a green and a maypole. On the wall of the Maypole Inn there is a complete list of licensees from Ambrose Wigglesworth in 1695 to Robert Palmer, who took over in 1983. For some reason the inn changed its name in about 1875 to the Eagle Hotel, but thought better of it in 1901 and became the Maypole again. Ambrose Wigglesworth doubtless approved of the return to tradition – if he knew about it. With a name like Wigglesworth – shared with a village only two miles away – his spirit seems unlikely to have wandered far.

Long Preston is on the legendary Settle-Carlisle route and has a tiny station with what look like bus shelters one on each side of the track. 'Access to Carnforth platform over the road bridge', a sign advises. That road bridge over the railway was obviously meant to last a thousand years, like everything else in Long Preston (more than once the winner of a 'best kept village' accolade). Much of the church, St Mary's, hidden at the end of a side road and surrounded by table tombs, has been here since the fourteenth century.

Standing at the junction of a side street with the main road, a man sees a car about to turn and utters a warning 'Hey up!' You feel that Long Preston has moved into the twentieth century with some reluctance.

A leaflet apparently published as a joint venture by the old LMS Railway and Settle Council in about 1925 proves that Settle, 'in the heart of Ribblesdale', was being promoted as a tourist area long before Dales folk became a popular theme of television drama serials.

The writer enthuses about the town as a centre for 'the new sports of pot-holing and rock-climbing', comparing its climbs with those of the Lake District and the Isle of Skye. And he reminds us of somebody's claim that 'the scenery around this quaint little town would have sufficed, if it had been on the continent . . . to make the reputation of a dozen villages'. A photograph showing a wide expanse of 'Settle Market Place and Shambles', an area now frequently packed with cars, reveals only four vehicles – one an ancient lorry. The peace of the scene, which for once affords an uninterrupted view of the Old Shambles with its graceful arches, might awaken envy in present-day residents.

It seems surprising how little of Settle was known by that copywriter in the twenties. He mentions the Shambles, but not Castleberg Crag, 300 feet high, or the seventeenth-century house called Preston's Folly, or Tot Lord, now dead, alas, who founded the famous Pig Yard Museum. He even left out the Ribblehead Viaduct, the titanic Victorian structure, whose passing thousands will mourn if British Rail finally closes it.

'Summer Tickets' to Settle were issued from LMS stations in 1925 – 'the charge is a penny a mile for the return journey . . . you can travel by any train you like, any day of the week, and stay away as long as you like up to a month. Moreover, you can break your journey anywhere you like en route, provided that the outward journey is completed within three days.'

Settle has had its distinguished visitors, including Queen Victoria and Edward Elgar, who loved it from the time he first visited a local GP, Dr Buck, a dedicated musician, who not only played the cello and the violin but collected local folk songs from long-memoried old characters like Betty Stockdale. Elgar harmonised several of these songs which Buck had recorded and arranged, and his much-loved *Salut d'Amour* was probably composed here. Walking and driving about Craven, the two men, who became lifelong friends, shared a fondness for 'japes' as well as their deepest thoughts about life and art. In 1885 Dr Buck presented Elgar with a terrier, Scap, which soon succumbed to the fragrant charms of a tripe shop near Elgar's home. 'It would do you good to see him skip into the shop and around the corner, and then fly out with the old woman after him,' wrote the composer to his friend.

The very name of Settle's near neighbour, Giggleswick, might have been expected to put a stop to any hope it might cherish of advancement in the serious world. Not a bit of it! The sixteenth century was no more than half-way through before Edward VI had granted a charter for the 'Gramer Schole' founded here in a cottage in 1512, which was to become one of the most famous public schools in England. It had Sir Matthew Smith, the Halifax-born painter, as a pupil and, more recently, Russell Harty as a master.

More tellingly, perhaps, it had as its patron Walter Morrison, of Malham Tarn House, famous for his friendship with Victorian lions such as Darwin and Charles Kingsley. Morrison it was who erected a school chapel to mark Victoria's Diamond Jubilee and suggested the chapel's copper roof, now blending with the green of the landscape. And it was Morrison's Giggleswickian idea to install a stained glass window representing five school worthies including the then head and the Rev. James Carr, founder of the school.

How typical it is of Giggleswick to have an 'ebbing and flowing well' at the foot of Buckshaw Brow, whose waters were said to rise and fall 'sometimes thrice in an hour'. I wonder if George Fox had time to reflect on these vagaries while in Giggleswick. Probably not, for he was imprisoned here in the village inn. It stands next to the fifteenth-century village church, St Alkelda's, though that can have been little consolation to Fox, who had small regard for 'steeple houses'. Inside the church, the knightly effigies have a Settle man's monument for company: he was Dr George Birkbeck, founder of the Mechanics Institute movement, in whom Fox might well have found a kindred spirit had they lived in the same century.

Giggleswick has a claim to geological fame in Giggleswick Scar, where the mid-Craven fault forms a wall of shining limestone skirting the A65 to Kirkby Lonsdale. There are man-made 'scars', too, caused by quarrying, but on the whole, Giggleswick's is a comely face, if a shy one, as it seems to hide in a hollow, its seventeenth-century houses clustering around the church as if seeking protection from the noisy modern world and the tourists who flock to and from Settle on their way up and down the dale.

Langcliffe, a mile to the north, was once renowned for the tanning of leather, though the most industrious – and certainly the noisiest – creatures here often appear to be the churchyard rooks. Gracious houses, old and new, surround the large, well-kept green. From the next village, Stainforth, a road sweeping eastward to Halton Gill in Littondale was once thronged with packhorses, for it was on an important route between Lancashire and the North-East. A packhorse bridge connecting Great and Little Stainforth may date back to the monks of Sawley Abbey, who probably built it. Below the bridge, the river diverts the onlooker with its antics at Stainforth Force.

The main road up the dale passes a side-turning to the left which leads into Crummackdale, yet another of the lesser dales that are so well worth exploring. It passes the hamlets of Wharfe and Austwick, from where a road leads northward to the geologically famous Norber boulders ('erratics' to the well-informed), many of which appear almost comically strange, balanced as they are on smaller rocks – reversals of the proverbial 'pea on a drum'. The reason, obvious now but undreamed of at one time, is that glaciers scattered these hard boulders on the softer underlying limestone, which eroded over the ages at a faster rate than the humpty dumpties perched upon it.

Clapham, a few miles to the west, is a shy village, hiding its greatest charms from visitors who see only the tidy car park and the Information Centre, where a pleasant blonde girl waited to answer varied queries about the valley of the Ribble and its neighbouring dales. A visitor entered clad in walking gear and expressing concern about a sheep in trouble. 'It's either ill or dying.' Once the blonde girl learned the sheep's whereabouts she knew exactly which farmer's wife to phone. The reply could be heard in the otherwise silent room – 'Thanks a lot, dear. 'Bye'.

There seemed to be few visitors that day – late autumn – though the dales were at their pastel-shaded best. The relief map of the Clapham area, the displays of photographs illustrative of dry stone walling and forestry, offered little competition to the late October sunshine and the gorgeous red-gold of the trees.

Clapham church has an early-fourteenth-century tower, which is said to have replaced an earlier one destroyed in a Scottish raid. In the church porch was displayed *The Story of the Witch of Clapham*, retold by Peter Winstone, then vicar, and apparently available from the vicarage.

I bought a copy and found that Mr Winstone writes in a style appropriately reminiscent of Charles Kingsley – 'This is a story about Clapham. Not the big sprawling Clapham in South London, famous for its railway junction, all soot and grime and flats and houses.' Nor, apparently the Clapham in Bedfordshire or Sussex, but 'the proper Clapham, the famous Clapham, the lovely Clapham, in fact the Yorkshire Clapham which is on the southern slopes of the famous mountain of Ingleborough, where is the famous Clapham Cave, and the famous Gaping Ghyll and the famous little rocky gorge called Trow Gill, and the little beck which laughs and makes a clapping noise as it runs over the stones through the village; and from that clapping sound the name of Clapham is said to come.'

The witch of the title was Dame Alice Ketyll, foster-mother of Sir John de Clapham who lived in Clapham Castle, while Dame Alice lived in a humble cottage at the foot of Trow Gill. Just why Dame Alice sold her soul to the devil I shall not tell you, nor what momentous events followed.

The path to the 'famous Clapham Cave' was closed – 'Shooting in Progress' read the notice, though we hardly needed to be told for the echoing bangs. The path would have led also to the Ingleborough Grounds Walk, a lake 200 yards away and to Ingleborough Hill itself, 2373 feet four miles away.

Ingleborough Hall, now an outdoor education centre, was once the home of Reginald Farrer, 'the Father of English Rock Gardening', whose rockery, rich in plants brought home from sometimes perilous globe-trotting was world-famous. He wrote such books as *The Rainbow Bridge* or *The Garden of Asia*. Flowers were named after him – *Lillium farreri* and *Gentiana farreri*. He was less than 40 when he died in 1920 while plant-hunting in Burma.

A few miles to the north-west lies Ingleton, whose claim to be the 'Beauty Spot of the North' (announced in large letters on a signpost) may seem a little unconvincing on a rainy day in late autumn, when the caravans look forlorn in the shadow of the railway viaduct. At such a time, other signposts directing you to The Waterfalls serve as reminders that Ingleton does have a more exciting side than it presents at first sight.

It must certainly have had a more obvious claim to beauty in 1769, when Thomas Gray, one of the few to discover it before the latter part of the last century, declared it to be a pretty village 'at the foot of that huge monster of nature – Ingleborough'.

However, despite the less lovely touches added since Gray's day, it could have been worse ... It could, for instance, have been a colliery village if the coal re-discovered there earlier this century had been continually exploited.

But if Ingleton is now (as Norman Duerden calls it in his *Portrait of the Dales*) a Beauty Spot without Beauty, its surroundings have remained at least as beautiful as they were when Ingleton first derived its name from the beacons which used to blaze, when national danger threatened, from the summit of Thomas Gray's 'huge monster'. It is easier indeed to write about Ingleborough than about Ingleton, even if the eighteenth-century botanist Tom Penny, hunting for cloud-berries on its slopes, exaggerated when he called it England's highest mountain. At 2373 feet it is in fact a little less than Whernside, highest of the famed Three Peaks. Yet it looks bigger; it is majestic and dramatic and it seems perfectly fitting that on this summit the northern tribes rallied to the Brigantian standard to resist the Romans.

Today, not only the northern, but the southern, western and eastern tribes rally to Ingleton, at holidays and weekends, to see the surrounding mountains but – more especially – those waterfalls and caves. They have been coming since an 'Improvement Association' (no doubt composed of comers-in) astonished the indigenous population by making the glens and waterfalls, hitherto largely ignored, accessible to the visiting public. Doubtless to an accompaniment of muted grumbling they laid paths and fixed handrails, made steps and footbridges. And they found an eager ally in the railway company, whose colourful posters blazoned Ingleton's fame abroad and who laid on special trains to bring the trippers. A hundred thousand of them came in 1893, chiefly to see the Falls Walk which still attracts its devoted admirers.

How they would gladden the hearts of those early publicists for whom Ribblesdale far outdid Naples – 'See Ingleton', they urged, 'and *then* die!'

Due east, and reachable only by doubling back on our tracks, or pressing forward and then completing a circuit, is Horton-in-Ribblesdale, which seems determined to associate itself with arduous physical exertion. Not only is it at the heart of the Three Peaks country which has attracted walkers and cyclists for generations, but it is a magnet for potholers.

The famed three peaks are Whernside, Penyghent and Ingleborough and if the first Three Peakers, as this elite fraternity call themselves, two teachers from Giggleswick School, could revisit the scene of their triumph they might wonder what they had started. For in late September, Horton becomes the centre of the amazing Three Peaks Cycle Race, described by its organizers as the world's toughest of its kind. Cyclists from all over Britain, as well as a Swiss team, regularly compete in this gruelling 50 kilometre contest, which involves so much more than mere cycling; for at least five miles of the circuit contestants have to carry or push their machines.

From Horton you may scale the heights or plumb the depths (though hardly on a bicycle . . . yet). Within easy striding distance of the village are such famous holes in the ground as Alum Pot (130 feet long by 40 wide and a dizzy-making 292 feet deep), Gingle Pot, Long Churn Hole, Hull Pot and Penyghent Hole, at 500 feet one of Yorkshire's deepest 'pots'.

If you love wildness, Ribblesdale will entrance you. The curlews and the lapwings call above the splash of falling water and the bleat of a distant sheep. Any link with the industrialism of the West Riding seems unlikely, and yet such a link exists in the form of Moughton Scar from which was quarried, in former days, the renowned Moughton whetstone greatly valued in Sheffield by the makers of razors.

Much of Horton was formerly owned by the monks of Jervaulx Abbey. A link with those medieval times is the fragmentary glass in the west window of St Oswald's, a handsome stone-built edifice with a Norman font and arcades.

My subject is villages, but he would be a blind guide who failed to remark the majesty of the road ahead. To the west, Penyghent rises 2273 feet, while eastwards, Ingleborough tops that by another hundred feet. Below ground there is scenery just as impressive for those venturesome and skilled enough to find it. No wonder man was challenged here to produce the grandeur of the Ribblehead viaduct.

To Chapel-le-Dale come the devotees of this colossus, anxious to photograph it while it still exists. The little, low church of St Leonard, which as a former chapel of ease gave the name Chapel-le-Dale to the village, has become a shrine to this marvel of Victorian engineering. For since 1876, when the Midland Railway Company placed a memorial on the wall to those whose lives had been given in the viaduct's building, this church has been linked with the structure. In the churchyard lie the bodies of an unnamed 200 who succumbed when smallpox raged through one of the shanty towns where the navvies who built the Settle-Carlisle line lived their rumbustious lives.

There is a seventeenth-century feel about this hamlet. The church – though partly rebuilt in 1869 – is essentially of an earlier date, like the Hill Inn, beloved of pot-holers and climbers. But the parish originally provided pasture for sheep kept here by the monks of Furness Abbey.

Almost due north of Chapel-le-Dale, Whernside's 2419 hulk announces that we are about to enter the so-called new county of Cumbria, though we are still in the Yorkshire Dales National Park. Between us, now, and our objectives, Dentdale and Garsdale, lies a waste (if that is not too harsh a word) of moorland and mountain – Scales Moor, Blea Moor and Deepdale, crossed by the Settle-Carlisle line. Running east and west, Dentdale follows the course of the River Dee from Stone House to Sedbergh, between Rise Hill (1825 feet) to the north and Whernside to the south. And we too will do well to follow it, for this route offers some of the loveliest country in the Dales.

Stone House . . . Cowgill . . . Dent . . . Of Cowgill we shall hear more, for this little place, with surely the humblest of names, once exercised the concern of England's Queen Empress and became the subject of a special Act of Parliament. And all because of one man's love for his native dale.

In 1985 Dent Town, as it is proud to call itself, held a festival to celebrate the bicentenary of the birth of its most remarkable product, Adam Sedgwick. His photograph, taken at the age of 83, beamed gently out from the Festival programme with the air of a man at peace with God and the world.

Many towns and villages have their very own great man commemorated by a pompous statue in a public park or a fading portrait hidden in the town hall. Sedgwick's memorial, on the other hand, carries the impact of an inspiration. In the old market place of Dent it stands, a great slab of Shap granite serving as a drinking fountain and inscribed simply *Adam Sedgwick 1785–1873*. Sedgwick has been called 'one of the best field geologists of all time', but he was much more than a geologist. A friend and collaborator of Wordsworth, he was, said Queen Victoria, to her 'an elder brother'.

Born on 22 March, the third child of the Rev. Richard Sedgwick, Perpetual Curate of Dent, Adam went from Dent Grammar School to Trinity College, Cambridge, with the intention of following his father into the Church, but under the spell of geology, won election to the vacant Woodwardian Professorship of Geology at Cambridge.

A friend and, later, an opponent of Darwin, he was concerned to harmonize the new discoveries with his Christian theology, but while his scientific theorizing may now seem to belong to a vanished age, his writings about his native village, *A Memorial by the Trustees of Cowgill Chapel (1868)* and *Supplement to the Memorial (1870)*, are among the classics of their genre.

Sedgwick himself had laid the foundation stone of the chapel in 1837. But the building was not properly registered and 30 years later a rash curate tried to change its name on the basis of what at first appeared to be some half-baked research, thus arousing the opposition of the 83-year-old geologist. A special Act of Parliament was needed to restore the name Cowgill to the chapel and Queen Victoria, no less, convinced by Sedgwick's arguments in his *Memorial* (unfounded as they turned out to be), declared herself on his side. The controversy itself, judged superficially, may seem to have been of little importance and some may marvel now that a man of his stature concerned himself with it. But he was, after all, a Dalesman and an old one at that, to whom his native village had become ever dearer with the passing years. Though the controversy which brought them to birth has long been forgotten, their vignettes of bygone Dales life ensured these privately printed memoirs a growing readership and a permanent place in rural literature. Here is Sedgwick describing the arrival of the news of the victory of Waterloo, first heralded by the sound of Sedbergh church bells ...

'Pray what means that ringing?' he said to a countryman.

'News, Sir, such as niver was heard before: I kna lile little about it; but the Kendal Postman had just come an hour before his time. He was all covered with ribbons and his horse was all covered with froth.'

Sedgwick put spurs to his horse and arrived in Sedbergh 'not many minutes after the arrival of the *Gazette Extraordinary* which told us of the great victory of Waterloo'.

'After joining in the cheers and gratulations of my friends at Sedbergh, I returned to Dent with what speed I could ... and then mounting on the great blocks of black marble, from the top of which my countrymen have so often heard the voice of the auctioneer and the town crier, I read, at the highest pitch of my voice, the news from the

Gazette Extraordinary to the anxious crowd which pressed round me. After the tumultuous cheers had somewhat subsided, I said, "Let us thank God for this great victory and let the six bells give us a merry peal."'

More often it is homelier matters that he describes – like the 'sittings' when a group of neighbours would gather in someone's house to knit. 'They took their seats; and . . . with a speed that cheated the eye they went on with their respective tasks. Beautiful gloves were thrown off complete; and worsted stockings made good progress. There was no dreary deafening noise of machinery; but there was the merry, heart-cheering sound of the human tongue. No one could foretell the current of the evening's talk. They had their ghost tales; and their love tales and their battles of jest and riddles; and their ancient songs of enormous length, yet heard by ears that were never weary . . .'

No town in England was more famous for its knitters – the 'terrible' (or marvellous) knitters of Dent as they were called in those days. The production by hand of woollen goods was a cottage industry of great importance hereabouts and the products of villages like Dent would be conveyed each week by packhorse to Kendal market.

Dent, says Sedgwick, 'was once a land of "statesmen"', the local name for small yeomen farmers. The village, or town, he knew, with its flats, linked by 'galleries', was by no means identical with the Dent we see today. Undoubtedly he idealized and sentimentalized the simple life and 'happy industry' of those he was bound to see as his inferiors. But he was not the only one who appeared to see Dent through a golden haze. In the 1830s William Howitt described a people whose rustic nobility was the cause of the failure of a cotton mill which someone briefly tried to run in Dent and which in Howitt's time stood as 'a ruinous monument' to the factory system. They loved 'the fresh mountain air' too much to put up with factory life. And 'the parents had too much love for their children to subject them to daily incarceration amid heat and dust and flue from the cotton.' And yet it was not from that mill, but from a knitting school in Dent itself that two little girls escaped, as Robert Southey records in his account of the 'terrible knitters', to be congratulated by those who gave them refuge, because Dent 'was t' poorest plaace in t'warld'. Perhaps it was. And yet it is easy to believe that there is something special about the place, as indeed there should be about a capital. For Dent was once the centre of an ancient kingdom bearing its name; though today its only 'kingdom' is the lovely little dale whose name it shares, the valley of the Dee.

This was marble-producing country, hence the marble chancel floor of St Andrew's Church, essentially unchanged from the church in which Adam's father preached. Sedgwick's *Memorial* contains many references to the former life of his native town, including its industries, which had included, besides farming and knitting, coal mining and quarrying. But in a footnote he admits, 'The fine marble works belong to this century and are better known to my countrymen than myself.

'Some years before I ever saw the light', he writes, 'there was an expected contest for the county of York. Mr Wilberforce [*the* William Wilberforce], a young man of bright presence and great eloquence, was then first named as a Candidate: and he had even then become famous as an enthusiastic advocate for the abolition of the Slave Trade. This fact set every chord of my father's heart in motion. He consulted his early friends, the good old Quakers in Kirthwaite; and his other friends in all the five hamlets, and he personally canvassed the valley from house to house ... and every vote was pledged for Mr Wilberforce. Soon afterwards came a Solicitor to canvass on the other side: but wherever he asked for a vote, the reply was, "*Nae use Sir, we o' here gang wi' the Parson.*"'

Today this little town, with its narrow twisted cobbled streets and white-washed houses set amid the smooth slopes of the Fells, bears the inevitable mark of tourism. I found a local shop selling miniatures of the Sedgwick memorial fountain and Sedgwick memorial plates, but, happily, such things do not detract from the unmistakable character of the village centre, apparently little changed since Sedgwick's time: both he and his father probably used the mounting steps at the Sun Inn.

3

By Wharfe and Nidd

HUMPTY DUMPTY AND EUGENE ARAM

Long before you reach Wharfedale and Otley on the journey from Leeds, you encounter village England at Adel, where Adel Crag inspired the young Henry Moore, the Castleford-born sculptor, to create his two-piece Reclining Figure in bronze.

Adel has a beautiful Norman church (much in demand for weddings) with a wondrously carved porch and an ancient bronze knocker, reminiscent of sanctuary days, on the door. Once, like other Leeds suburbs – Alwoodley, Whitkirk and Kirkstall (home to the industrious but now ruined abbey that foreshadowed Leeds) – the village was a place of importance in the old Brigantian kingdom of Elmete.

But where, precisely, does Wharfedale itself begin? My choice is Cawood, where the gatehouse of Cawood Castle, built of the same creamy white limestone as York Minster, recalls the splendid state in which archbishops of York, notably Cardinal Wolsey, used to live before the time of the present archiepiscopal palace at Bishopthorpe.

Here, Wolsey, 'the Mitred peacock', as he was called by Mother Shipton, the Knaresborough prophetess, in one of her more probable utterances, was arrested for high treason, having shown too little enthusiasm in helping Henry divorce Catherine of Aragon to marry Anne Boleyn. The cardinal died at Leicester on his way to stand trial and demonstrating, according to Shakespeare, a noble acceptance of the fate he felt he so little deserved –

> Had I but served my God with half the zeal
> I served my king, he would not in mine age
> Have left me naked to mine enemies.

A less reverent version of his downfall is supposedly contained in the nursery rhyme about Humpty Dumpty and his great fall!

Did the villagers of Cawood care much about the machinations of kings and prelates? Perhaps not. It may be true or merely a sentimental legend that Cawood folk shed tears as their local notable was led away – to death, as they doubtless thought. He is reputed to have won their affections, and being human, they probably felt a wondering pride that their village was home to a man second in power only to the King himself. But perhaps Cawood folk were less easily moved to tears than the pious legend suggests.

Nevertheless, Cawood has a 'watery' character! The Ouse, joined just north of here by the Wharfe, is sprinkled with boats, but the village is still primarily agricultural – the erstwhile palace, with its beautiful oriel windows, is hemmed in by farm buildings and from the iron bridge sugar beet barges may be seen on the river which bore the Viking sea raiders to York. Ancient Ryther and Ulleskelf, a little way upstream, seem unimpressed by the presence, just a few miles away at Selby, of Britain's new and technologically advanced coal mine.

Here, south of York and north-east of Leeds, the green landscape is spotted with grey stone villages – Appleton Roebuck, Acaster Malbis, Wistow, Kelfield. At Nun Appleton Hall, Bolton Percy, lived the archetype of the English gentleman, Thomas Fairfax, Cromwell's leading general, who nevertheless helped to restore the Stuart reign when he was convinced that England once more needed a king.

Follow a winding road northward and you reach Bilbrough, where, on Ingrish Hill, swarthy Fairfax ('Black Tom') would sit remembering battles fought and won . . . kings and common soldiers, his children and his much-loved wife who slept now in the little church at Bilbrough. It would not be long before he joined her, as he had made sure he would by the wording of his will.

Ingrish Hill . . . a fitting place for an old war horse to sit and ponder. How his interest would have quickened had he learned that many years later the remains would be found of a beacon, one of a chain that would blaze in warning should the country be invaded by Napoleon. Bilbrough's parish registers record the baptism of a child of one George Teazle, 'a soldier at the beacon', in 1808.

Thomas, third Baron Fairfax, born at Denton Hall, near Otley (though the house that stands there today was rebuilt in the eighteenth century) retired, when he thought his active life was over, to Nun Appleton lower down the dale in the hope of peace at last among his books and other treasures. And it was to Nun Appleton Hall that Andrew Marvell came as tutor in languages to Black Tom's daughter Maria, and here he wrote some of his finest poems.

Had Fairfax been born and raised closer to the capital he might have been better remembered. Not that the modest Thomas would pine for posthumous fame: genuinely retiring by nature, his spirit must have stammered a protest when a fund was started recently to restore his tomb in the south chapel of Bilbrough Church.

At Church Fenton, south-east of Towton where a great battle was fought in 1461, weapons far deadlier than Yorkist arrows thrill great crowds on a Sunday in June when R.A.F. Church Fenton holds an air display. If you love aircraft and the noise they make and the crowds they attract, you will love this. If not, visit instead Sherburn-in-Elmet, a couple of miles to the south where, even on the great day, the sound of the engines will be somewhat muffled.

Is Sherburn village or town? It has aspects of both, with farms and red pantiled roofs, as well as modern, brick-built shops and old pubs with names like the Red Bear or the White Swan. Here and there are hints of its former greatness, for Sherburn was the Brigantian kingdom of Elmet's eastern capital, while Barwick-in-Elmet was its capital-in-chief.

The hill on which stands All Saints' Church was crowned by an earlier church, but that Saxon structure could hardly have matched the majesty of the present, largely Norman building in white limestone. Nor, perhaps, had it so intriguing a history. For here, in 1321, a secret conclave of clergy and barons met to protest against the misrule of Edward II. Here, also in secret, worshipped Roman Catholics in time of persecution.

Made from the same limestone as the church is the Janus Cross, dating back perhaps six hundred years. Buried during the Reformation, it was rediscovered in the nineteenth century, when much controversy ensued as to its ownership. Surprisingly, the cross was then sawn vertically into halves and both faces of Janus can now be seen mounted in the south aisle.

Archbishops of York used to have a palace at Sherburn, given to them by the Anglo-Saxon King Athelstan. Today, only a few mounds in a field to the north of the church remain to mark the site of archiepiscopal splendour.

Tadcaster ('Taddy' to its friends and residents) is no village, but a busy town of pubs and brewery chimneys. Not everyone appreciates Taddy; even those who live there have been known to complain that it is drabber than need be. But for everyone who complains, there are three to take up verbal cudgels on their home town's behalf. Not that all Tad's residents are ferocious. The very largest of them are perhaps the gentlest – splendid grey brewery shires, each weighing a ton, which frequently plod along the main street, crossing the Wharfe by a five-arched bridge. From the bridge built, in its original narrower form, in the seventeenth century, you can see the lovely white limestone church of St Mary. Once it stood nearer the Wharfe but was so vulnerable to flooding when the waters rose that in 1877 it was taken to pieces and rebuilt out of the river's reach. Tadcaster, midway between Leeds and

York on the A64, links city and country, industrial and agricultural, ancient and modern and a multitude of villages surrounds it and dots the course of the Wharfe.

We are still in Fairfax country. The great parliamentary family is rarely more palpably present than at Newton Kyme, where lived Admiral Robert Fairfax in a pillared hall graced by avenues of lime trees first planted on his orders. Robert, as much a fighter as the illustrious 'Black Tom', took part in the capture of the Rock of Gibraltar in 1704, which fact is recalled on his memorial tablet in the village church, St Andrew's, by a fully rigged ship. But keep away from Newton Kyme at Hallowe'en, for that's when Black Tom Fairfax rides between the limes to visit his kinsfolk!

A few miles west of Newton Kyme, Clifford has a French air befitting its 'Catholic' history, lit by folk memories of miracles at a 'holy well'. From a distance, its mysterious, alien effect is conveyed first of all by the tower (modelled on that of Angoulême Cathedral) of the Roman Catholic church of St Edward King and Confessor. Built around the 1850s, the project showed that Clifford could command support from some surprising and impressive patrons, including the Queen of France, the Duke of Parma and the King of Sardinia. Hardly surprising, then, that the local Catholic gentry, such as the Vavasours of Hazlewood Castle, now the home to a monastic community, were eager to demonstrate their piety and generosity.

St Edward's has stained glass windows by Pugin, though the rounded pillars carved by local masons have been praised as its greatest glory. But if Clifford folk (among others) have willingly given of their money and their skill for their religion, when it came to sterner trials, in 1569, they showed no enthusiasm to join the ill-fated Rising of the North. They were no more inclined to warfare when the Royalists came looking for soldiers during the Civil War.

The 'holy well', with its pointed roof over an archway containing a doorway blocked with stone, was once a baptismal well, I was told by a man scything nettles. There were plans to restore it, he said, but initial moves had been complicated by the apparent absence of an owner.

You could easily forget nearby Bramham's situation just off the A1 were it not for the muffled roar of traffic from that thunderous thoroughfare. Even with that inescapable background, the village – at least in its oldest parts – strikes the motorist suddenly as almost unbelievably delightful. Its ochre-walled houses, topped with red pantiles, suggest the North York Moors rather than Lower Wharfedale.

History is in the air at Bramham. A Roman road crosses the path of the A1 – on Bramham Moor in 1408 a bloody battle was fought – fine old houses and halls seem to confront you at every turn. All Saints'

Church, surrounded by venerable tombstones of long-dead villagers, combines Norman and early English work.

Synonymous with Bramham is the splendid home of the Lane Fox family, descendants of Robert Benson, First Lord Bingley, who built it. He was an ambassador and a courtier to Queen Anne, who gave her name to the architectural style Bramham Park so worthily typifies. In 1828 fire so damaged the house that it remained unoccupied for 78 years, though for all that time the gardens were tended. Today, 250 years after they were laid out, those gardens still owe their shape to their original inspiration – French gardens like those at Versailles, complete with ornamental lakes and ponds, walks, vistas and avenues. In 1962 gales uprooted 400 mature trees, necessitating much re-planting.

One resident of Bramham who knew the village both before and after the building of the house (1699–1710) and who was almost as much a wonder in his own way, was Levi Whitehead, who won renown as the fastest runner in England. Levi once clocked four miles in 19 minutes. The exercise clearly agreed with him, for he was still walking four miles a day when he was 96 and he had reached a hundred when he died in 1787.

These Lower Wharfedale villages represent a facet of rural life without which Yorkshire would lack some of its infinite variety.

At Thorp Arch, opportunism has prevented stagnation. An enormous wartime munitions factory now serves as a trading estate and shopping centre which brings visitors from a wide area. Even more surprising is the presence, near this village of creeper-clad cottages around a delightful green, of the British Library (Lending Division), opened in 1962 as the National Lending Library for Science and Technology. Here is housed Britain's largest loan collection of the world's scientific literature, supplied by a postal loan service to United Kingdom organizations.

Boston Spa ('Spaw' in the venacular of the elderly) is one of the many Yorkshire towns and villages which enjoyed a passing fame for the allegedly health-giving properties of their waters. It was in fact the discovery of a chalybeate spring that brought the town to birth in the Georgian era, when its main purpose was to cater for the rheumatism sufferers who came to the Wharfe Valley to seek relief.

It was an age when the discoverers of medicinal waters seem to have achieved quite inordinate fame. Ann Farrow is remembered for discovering the waters of Scarborough and William Slingsby, for performing a similar service for Harrogate. And it was one John Shires, of nearby Thorp Arch, whose recommendations brought the sufferers to Boston Spa. At one time there were seven wells here – the Crown Hotel, dating from the 1750s, stands on the site of one of them – and who knows what might have become of Boston Spa had not Queen Victoria bestowed royal patronage on Harrogate instead?

That indefatigable wanderer Edmund Bogg, who, between working at his picture-framing business in Leeds, cycled about the countryside in the 1900s, dutifully followed by his illustrator, was fulsome in his praise of Boston Spa, then renowned for the longevity of its inhabitants – there were at least two centenarians and quite a few had *almost* clocked up the hundred before departing, one hopes, for more truly paradisal realms. In those days the Spa Baths Refreshment Rooms (as advertised in Bogg's book, along with his picture-framing business) catered for small parties (home-made cakes and pastries, pleasure boats for hire) and sold spa water at a penny a glass.

Not all that long ago I found you could still buy a glass of spa water at what remained of the old Spa Baths. 'I've drunk gallons of it,' I was told by the lady who issued it with the aid of a beer pump installed for the purpose when the original pump broke down. 'Very good for curing spots'.

Doubtless Boston Spa has changed since Bogg's day. Today it seems all smart shops and offices, restaurants and estate agents with a sprinkling of antique and picture galleries. Perhaps it was never a village in the old, slow-growing but enduring sense, but a boom town, which missed the bus caught by Harrogate and, thanks to its lovely surroundings and convenient proximity to the A1, caught another, the Commuter Belt Special, whose passengers often speak with accents that would fall strangely on the ears of John Shires of neighbouring Thorp Arch, who first discovered the health-giving waters.

The surrounding countryside hereabouts is studded with innumerable villages whose claim to notice is out of all proportion to their size. Thorner, for instance, for a time the home of the poet R.C. Scriven (Ratz to his friends and old *Punch* readers), who used to meet me at the Fox for memorable if laborious lunches; for Ronald Scriven was both blind and deaf and though some could talk to him, uncannily, in a barely raised voice, I was not so gifted, though I counted the effort a small price to pay for the privilege of his company. From his modest cottage he would tap his way unerringly to the bar, and locals and visitors who had often not read a line of poetry since leaving school would order, unheard by him, drinks he had to fumble for as a beatific smile of gratitude lit up the puckish features beneath that great, spreading brow.

Left an orphan at an early age, he was brought up in another Wharfedale village by a farming couple whose nicknames are almost a novel in themselves – Slow Joe and Iron Anne. Cosmopolitan and countryman, Ratz was compensated for the hammer blows dealt him by fate in the possession of a memory for sights and sounds which seemed to grow ever more vivid with the passing years. If he achieved his greatness because of, or despite, his limitations, I shall never know. Infirmities increased (as if he had not enough) with age, but still he lived into his seventies – no great age, that, in Thorner, however, where the numerous ancients used to hold their own marbles championship. Perhaps this pastime ensured the longevity of such as John Philips, who, according to an inscription in the chancel of Thorner church, was born in 1625 and died 117 years later.

The Wharfedale air *must* encourage longevity! When I first met him, many years ago at East Keswick, Owen Bowen was already 87 and still painting with amazing vigour. He had then been hung in 40 Royal Academy exhibitions and two years before we met he had held an exhibition in Collingham village under the title 'Seventy years of Painting' which attracted 3000 visitors, one of them a critic who declared that Bowen's oil of Meanwood Beck, painted when he was 15, showed 'all the assurance of one of the Dutch masters'.

For many years he had lived at neighbouring Collingham, where St Oswald's Church contains a rare circular cresset stone with eight hollows for oil lights, as well as fragments of ninth-century crosses. Linton, across the river, was chosen by the National Town Planning Council as an excellent example of good rural development, largely due to the houses designed by a Leeds firm of architects, whose senior partner was William Alban Jones, one of an artistic coterie that included Owen Bowen.

Was there a village at Harewood before Edwin Lascelles commissioned John Carr, 'the architect of the North', to build the Corinthian mansion Harewood House, and Capability Brown to surround it with gardens 'romantic' enough to incorporate the actual castle ruins? Yes, if we draw conclusions from the fact that the castle is Norman and Harewood Church, is mostly fifteenth-century. Both castle and church awaken distant echoes. The deposed King of Scotland, John Balliol, found refuge here for a time. It was his friend, Sir William Aldbergh, who enlarged the pile, perhaps to make it more fitting for its royal refugee. But time has dealt no less harshly with the castle for having been home to a king, and visitors nowadays are warned not to climb on its crumbling walls.

Harewood's church of All Saints has more tangible ghosts in the shape of a famous collection of alabaster monuments. No fewer than six recumbent couples sleep on tomb chests as they await eternity.

John Carr built not only the house, but most of the authentic village. Local stone was used to create a terrace and blocks of cottages along the approach to the main gates of the great house. One terrace of houses was designed as a ribbon factory to provide employment for the villagers. Carr built in 1760 but in the early nineteenth century front gardens were added under the influence of the landscaping vogue then current.

From Harewood, the A659 leads to Arthington and Nunnery Farm. There is no nunnery here now, for the Cluniac retreat founded by Peter de Arthington was dissolved in 1540. The fine old house in whose name the dispossessed sisters are remembered was built less than 50 years later. Its top 'windows' used to be 'glazed' with slate to escape the window tax but now they admit the light through ordinary glass.

To the north an abundance of villages between the Wharfe and the Nidd offers plenty to detain you: Huby, Leathley, Rigton. Above them rises the modest 600 foot eminence of Almscliff Crag with its tale of a lovelorn maiden's suicide attempt foiled by her crinoline. Further west, the River Washburn links a chain of reservoirs as it runs south from its moorland birthplace, passing West End, where now the old church lies beneath the waters, Blubberhouses, whose name has strained many an imagination and breezy Timble. There, in 1825, the village cobbler, William Holmes, was haunted by a tidy-minded spirit who collected up every scrap of leather nightly and put them all in the glue tin, on top of which it always laid two crossed strips of leather. No lock or bolt could keep it out. The only other sign of its presence was a sound of 'short' quick breathing. Unnerved by this unsought help, Holmes left cobbling and found much success as farmer and cattle dealer. So if the unseen visitant were indeed, as some said, the ghost of an idiot boy called Tommy Kaye, Holmes had much to thank him for . . .

The Wharfe has almost reached Otley (birthplace of Thomas Chippendale) when it passes between Leathley and Farnley, where Turner loved to stay with the squire and paint the Wharfedale scene.

North of the river, running parallel with the main road from Otley to Ilkley, a country road takes you pleasantly by way of Weston, Askwith and Denton (birthplace of Black Tom Fairfax) to Ilkley. Equally appealing is a moorland road south of the river, which goes by way of Burley Woodhead, where Job Senior, the sooth-saying, weather-forecasting hermit, is depicted in the colourful sign of the hospitable Hermit Inn.

Burley Woodhead rises to the moor from Burley-in-Wharfedale, which, with its rows of neat stone houses, has an air of tidy Victorian respectability. Burley has apparently inspired no masterpieces of literature, yet Charles Dickens could well have found a subject for his pen in the conditions of children employed here in two cotton mills; while the Brontës might have written about the fear inspired by the Luddites, which led to iron doors being fitted to mill workers' cottages – hence Iron Row, still to be found here.

Before any of that, Shakespeare would surely have rejoiced in the

Burley Great Pudding, a giant concoction of fruit and pastry that was boiled beneath the Pudding Tree between the Malt Shovel Inn and St Mary's Church and shared by all comers. The tree is dead now, but a successor grows from a flower bed on the site.

The last pudding was boiled in 1787, when Job Senior, the hermit of Burley Woodhead, was aged about seven. But even in Job's day, Burley was ancient. Mentioned in the Saxon Chronicle in 972, it was possibly an outpost on the Roman road running through well-wooded country from Adel to Ilkley. In 1822 Burley had a population of 1200, many of whom were children who worked in the two cotton mills. It seems odd that most of them came here from London to be fed and housed in a specially erected building until they had served their apprenticeships. By that time they were sufficiently 'naturalized' to settle in the place.

Beyond Ilkley the landscape opens out as we head for the real dales country and we can sense a freshness in the air. Ahead lie some of the finest villages in Yorkshire, such as Bolton Abbey. The village takes its name from what was, in fact, a priory, until Henry VIII got his hands on it on 29 January 1538, when Prior Richard Moone handed over the keys to the king's officers.

If the worthy Prior haunts the scenes of his earthly life he should be quite a happy spectre. As long ago as 1520 he commissioned the building of the west tower of the Priory Church. It was to have been a magnificent, soaring structure and, when it was completed, was to be linked with the church by the removal of the then existing west front. Sadly the Prior's intentions were frustrated by the monarch's greed, and for four centuries the tower remained half-finished, exposed to the worst the Wharfedale weather could do.

Then, in about 1980, an appeal was launched for £300 000 to complete the tower (not, however, quite as Prior Moone had intended, for his proposed tower would have been three times the height of the present edifice). Glass doors at the tower entrance allow a view of the church while the tower's west window is clear glazed to match the west window of the church.

That window was last glazed in 1884 at a cost of £21: the glazing costs involved in the renovation were £4000. Changes in money values over the centuries have become something of vulgar marvels in these inflationary times, yet we can hardly refrain from exclaiming over the fact that the £7 13s 4d left by John Yeoman of Appletreewick in 1535 'for the building of the steeple at Bolton Abbey' was in those days the price of 20 heifers or 160 sheep.

Bolton Priory forms part of the Yorkshire estate of the Duke of Devonshire, whose most famous property is the magnificent Chatsworth House in Derbyshire. The Duke's Yorkshire home, Bolton Hall, incorporates the old priory gatehouse and is largely built of stones from the ruins. But it is not only the gatehouse that continues to fill a human need, for the nave of the priory church is still used by the villagers as their parish church.

A day is hardly long enough to explore this favourite among Yorkshire beauty spots. If you can tear yourself away from the priory's idyllic riverside setting (and the children from their paddling and exertions on the ancient stepping stones), there is the Valley of Desolation to explore a little way upstream, with its memories of a cataclysmic storm. There are nature trails and, two miles from the priory, its sister ruin, Barden Tower, with other memories of the Shepherd Lord, Henry Clifford.

Popular as Bolton Abbey is today, there are older residents who remember it as an even greater draw. That was when the roads from Bolton Abbey railway station were 'black with people' and horses and wagonettes stood in line to take tourists to the Abbey or the Strid (stride), that deep and narrow part of the Wharfe which has tempted many to try to step across. It has cost many lives, including that of Wordsworth's 'Boy of Egremond', whose death, according to legend, led to his grief-stricken mother, Alice de Romilly, founding the Priory. A romantic tale, but no more, though it serves as a useful warning of the dangers of the Strid, from whose waters a white horse is said to arise whenever the water claims a victim.

In August the late King George V would arrive for the shooting. The village was alive, then, with detectives and equerries and the shooting party, with ponies and beaters and 12 guns and a loader for each guest, resembled a small army.

A little way up-dale stands Appletreewick, looking as though it has hardly changed for centuries. The old houses, Monk's Cottage, Mock Beggar Hall (tantalising names that partially reveal and partially hide the village's history) seem anxious to hide from view such modern houses as there are.

For all its present quietude, Appletreewick has seen busier times. Onion Lane there takes its name from the Onion Fair which once made it famous. On the rising land behind the village, lead was once mined, but you would need to look hard for signs of such industry today.

Until recently, Appletreewick's New Inn announced itself proudly as 'the only non-smoking licensed premises in England'. Had you failed to see the notice and proceeded to light your pipe or cigarette in John Showers's pub you could very likely have been invited to take his cure for smokers, holding a mouthful of pink liquid while listening to mine host's emotional recitation of his poem describing with deep sincerity the death from lung cancer of a dear friend.

Whether or not the 'cure' invariably succeeded, there can be no doubt that John Showers has been the most passionate of anti-nicotine campaigners, with a huge list of grateful patients he had rescued from the pernicious weed. It was no doubt in that same crusading spirit that he once poured a pint over the head of a defiant smoker who blew smoke in his face. Until illness intervened, John would show you, with some pride, his future tomb, at the top of the garden behind the pub, built of local stone and surmounted by growing flowers. It bears the inscription: *Erected in 1981 to commemorate the tenth anniversary of No Smoking at the New Inn.*

But I can hardly wait, now, to renew acquaintance with Burnsall, village of happy memory, where I was granted the truly 'signal' honour of starting the Burnsall Fell Race! Its official programme was adorned with a line-drawing showing the village as artists and photographers love to depict it, with its five-arched bridge spanning the Wharfe and the Church of St Wilfrid rising against its backcloth of hills. The church takes its name from the St Wilfrid whose feast is celebrated every August at Ripon, to which tiny city he returns to ride by proxy on a white horse as he leads a varied and colourful procession through the ancient streets.

Long ago – no-one knows exactly when – St Wilfrid, then Abbot of Ripon, visited Burnsall when it probably had no church at all and, as a result, a little wooden structure arose – nothing like so grand as the present church with its square tower, added in the sixteenth century. And Burnsall's stone church has changed its form many times since the Romilly family founded it soon after the Conquest. Its most famous restoration was by William Craven, born nearby at Appletreewick, who left the dale to make his fortune in the capital and in 1598, when he was 50, was made Lord Mayor of London. He also built the present village school and rebuilt Burnsall bridge.

But for all his fame, Sir William (as he became) never started the Fell Race, for it began only in about 1870, being born, as so many good things are, in the village pub, the Red Lion.

It was Tom Weston, who, after that seminal meeting, in the Red Lion, tried out the course of the first Burnsall Fell Face, running naked and by moonlight. Thereafter the Fell Race became an indispensable feature of Burnsall Feast and one which forever after has inspired local scribes to new heights of descriptive prose.

In the first report of the event, which appeared in the *Craven Herald* in 1882, one competitor, 'psyching' himself like any modern Olympic contestant, was seen before the start, 'bounding about as though he had been to the india-rubber factory and received a coating of that elastic ingredient' as he confidently declared to all within earshot that he would be the undoubted winner.

The race starts at Burnsall Green, 473 feet above sea level, and from there the runners push themselves up the well-nigh vertical fell-side until they reach a cairn of piled stones at 1345 feet – not quite the summit, which is another 300 feet or so higher.

Both amateur and professional 'times' are recorded for this event, as are 'ascent' and 'descent' times. In 1910, one E.H. Dalzell (from Cumbria, alas) electrified the dale by doing it in an incredible 12.59.8.

Was it really possible to return a time like that without resorting to flight – surely against the rules! Every August the wrangling was revived. Had Dalzell really done it – and if so, how? For years after, no-one came near Dalzell's record, thus almost confirming the doubters in their belief that such a time was impossible. Then in 1977, R. Wilde of Manchester Harriers achieved a time of 12 minutes 50 seconds and in a 'Jubilee' race the same year, R. Reeves recorded a professional time of 12.47.2.

Wilde's near namesake, J.R. Wild of the Cumberland Fell Runners, not only beat the Manchester runner in 1983 by achieving a time of 12.48, but that year saw him complete a hat trick with his third consecutive victory.

But there's more to Burnsall Feast Sports than the Classic Fell Race or its junior version for runners between 12 and 16, who must climb about 1000 feet to the Fell Gate. There's clay pigeon shooting, cycle racing and the Burnsall Morris Dancers, who, as like as not, will recall the shade of the Barguest, a monstrous hound that legend says once haunted Trollers Ghyll, a nearby valley with steep, enclosing hillsides.

If any part of Wharfedale can be called its 'heart', it must lie somewhere among a cluster of villages comprising Thorpe, Linton, Threshfield, Grassington and Hebden.

Thorpe almost succeeds in hiding itself, hence its full title, Thorpe-in-the-Hollow. They say that the Burnsall maypole once vanished from the green and was found at Thorpe after the infuriated Burnsall men had searched every other village around. Thorpe they had completely overlooked until they saw the maypole's gilded tip glinting in the sun.

Neolithic men hid in its so-called Fairy Caves in one of the many hills. Later, Dales folk hid there, with their cattle, from the raiding Scots. It is said the marauders never discovered Thorpe, let alone the Fairy Cave. Its other name was Navvy Noodle Hole and long before man discovered it, it was a refuge, as their remains have testified, for animals no longer seen in this or any land.

According to legend, this was a village of cobblers whose boots and shoes were famed throughout the dale. Respected authorities have stated that at one time there were as many as 40 following their trade here.

Was it really Sir John Vanbrugh who designed the Fountaine Hospital that looks benignly out on the green at Linton? The many-sided genius who built Castle Howard, that 'fortified town', as Horace Walpole called it, might well have drawn the lines for this miniature masterpiece, for Richard Fountaine, whose memorial it is, was Vanbrugh's timber merchant. At any rate, legend gives Vanbrugh the credit. Fountaine was a 'rural Dick Whittington' who left the Dales to make his fortune and returned to dispense their bounty.

Founded and endowed in 1721 to accommodate six poor men or women, the hospital contains a chapel in its central block, over which rises a square tower and cupola. In the wings are the almshouses themselves. Dales folk may be conservative by nature, but they are ready to copy what they really admire, which is why the Georgian grace and symmetry of the hospital began to find echoes in houses elsewhere in the Dales.

The Linton Beck, which bisects the green, has a plenitude of crossings – three bridges, besides stepping stones and fords. The bridges (a modern road bridge besides clapper and packhorse bridges) might have been placed there to illustrate the Evolution of The Bridge, and one of them, Lile Emily's Bridge, cries out for a story I have yet to hear.

Who was Lile (or little) Emily and what befell her at her quaint little hump-backed bridge? Since it dates perhaps from the fourteenth century it is hardly surprising if the story has long been forgotten.

Anything less like the 'mill-town' of popular imagination than this idyllic village it is hard to conceive, yet, like certain other Dales villages, Linton *was* a centre of the woollen trade. As late as 1959 Linton Mill was engaged in textile manufacture. The first Linton Mill, which ground corn, was rebuilt to make worsted cloth. Some cottages, named Botany, gained their name from Botany wool, and were built to house mill workers. The mill's varied life, which survived a fire, included a period as a creamery. It was last used for weaving cotton and rayon before it closed its doors for the last time.

Linton might be the perfect village, unless you feel that the holder of that title must contain a church. Linton's church hides a mile from the village on what some say was a pagan site, hence its protective dedication to the warrior prince of angels, St Michael, and his cohorts.

There is nothing grandiose about St Michael's. Long and low, with a square thirteenth-century bell turret as its nearest approach to a tower, it uses a pre-Reformation stone altar discovered at a time of restoration in 1861. The church has been enlarged and altered several times since the earliest surviving Norman work (in the north aisle of the nave) was completed, but the result has a harmony in keeping with the beautiful surroundings.

A relic of the earliest days is the Norman tub font. Weight alone makes it unlikely that this will follow out of the church a much more highly prized feature, a little brass ninth-century crucifix which was displayed, too trustingly as it proved, on one of the aisle pillars. Probably of continental origin, it was found in 1835 in Linton Beck. From 1905 it hung safely, in easy reach of anyone who paused to read what was known of its story on a brass plate beneath. Then, in 1981, someone reached out and wrenched it from its slender anchorage. Today a photograph of the lost treasure occupies its site on the pillar.

Perhaps a mile north of Linton, Threshfield has a glory to rival the Fountaine Hospital – its seventeenth-century Free Grammar School, founded by Matthew Hewitt, a one-time rector of Linton. It is a grammar school no longer – but a happy primary school. I hope it still survives and will long do so, for the sake of the children lucky enough to study in this superb example of Dales architecture with its mullioned windows and a two-storey gabled porch, the upper floor of which has a stepped three-light window.

There's always 'a trip in' at Grassington, or so you might think. Coaches pack the car park and cars fill the cobbled square, while crowds throng the main street, passing the shops selling fancy goods, crafts, knitwear and sheepskin, and the fruit shop with its plaque recalling the days when Tom Lee's 'smiddy' stood here.

Lee was the ill-natured blacksmith hanged at York for the murder of the much-loved Dr Petty, who had dared to reprove him for his evil ways.

A door in Garrs Lane, bearing a plaque reading Theatre Cottage, recalls the Grassington Theatre (it began life as a barn) whose boards once felt the tread of luminaries like Harriet Mellor and Edmund Kean. Their memory recalls a much more recent playwright and actor, Dick Gregson, whom I visited on one occasion at Grassington, where he used to live and where he was the natural choice as president of the Grassington Players.

No doubt if Dick still lived here he would play a lively part in the Grassington Festival, advertised in shop and post office windows. But if Dick Gregson was unable to take part, the name of another of my Grassington friends leaps out from the poster, that of Ronald Harker. He left the Dales to become foreign news editor of the *Observer*, then, in retirement, returned, as dalesmen so often do. His part in the festival was a lecture on 'A Dalesman's Diaries', based on an unpublished journal which I was once privileged to read.

An estate agent's window here contains evidence of the current boom in Dales properties at Langcliffe, Lothersdale, Skipton, Austwick ... Prices are well above the £50 000 mark for cottages, farm houses and barns that once might have gone for a thousand or two. A village inn is on offer for £197 500.

Across the cobbled square, once the market place, is the Upper Wharfedale Museum, 'a registered charity run by volunteers', and filled with a most engaging and varied collection of bygones.

Grassington presents the sturdy, affluent appearance of a well-loved, much-visited community, well aware of its attractions and including people of vigour and promotional zeal in their untiring work for the Yorkshire Dales Tourist Association. Much of Grassington's stability is an inheritance from the prosperous days of lead-mining on Grassington Moor, which ceased over a century ago. Though many left the Dales in search of new jobs, those who weathered out the storm and the century found that the opening of the Yorkshire Dales Railway between Skipton and Grassington in 1901 brought visitors, money and jobs back to the village.

Conistone follows the familiar Wharfedale village pattern, with limestone cottages roughly grouped around a green. Surrounding fields are marked on their lower slopes by the 'lynchet' terraces left by Anglian farmers. Seventeenth- and eighteenth-century cottages have been converted to modern dwellings, yet Conistone is one of Wharfedale's least spoilt villages and credited with a most harmonious if mysterious name meaning *Conyng's* (or king's) tune. Less poetic but possibly more plausible is the version 'King's enclosure', for Domesday Book records that these lands were once held by the king's thanes. Conistone's church, St Mary's, is reputedly the oldest in Craven, founded in Saxon times.

The village might well seem asleep, except at haytime. It rests from the busy life that ended in the sixteenth century. Before then it had the milling of Fountains Abbey's corn and was thronged with traffic from the abbey's grange at Kilnsey.

Travellers in Wharfedale for the first time are invariably impressed by Kilnsey Crag, a huge jutting cliff of limestone which dominates the landscape and provides a superb backcloth for one of the most delightful events in the Pennine Dales – Kilnsey Show.

If you want to see the village show par excellence, come to Kilnsey at August Bank Holiday, when the flat bottom of the Wharfe valley is bright with marquees and caravans and horse boxes. Men wise in the ways of dogs and sheep lean their elbows on pens and study their woolly tenants. Elsewhere, other men concentrate intensely on the titivation of magnificent heavy horses. And in the great oval show ring, a cattle class is being solemnly judged, the animals as spotless as the gleaming white coats of the stockmen whose responsibility shows in every line of their bronzed or ruddy faces.

What began on 7 September 1897 as the little show hesitantly staged by the newly formed Wharfedale Agricultural Society, with entries of

75 sheep, 51 cattle and 31 horses plus the inevitable exhibitions of butter and cheese, now attracts perhaps 16 000 visitors whose cars pack fields earmarked for that purpose along the Skipton and Kettlewell road. Happily, they are not close enough to the actual site of the show to detract from the picture it presents in its setting between Wharfe and Crag. The crag, incidentally, becomes a star exhibit of the day when it features in the race up and down its rocky contours which has taken place since 1899.

Just a couple of miles north of Kilnsey the River Skirfare, whose name means 'Bright Stream', loses its identity in the Wharfe. From its birth out of the side of Penyghent it runs its little course – ten miles, if that – through a dale which surely does its best to hide from the traffic purposefully thronging the main Wharfedale highway.

That dale is Littondale. Well over a century ago, Charles Kingsley came here from Malham Tarn House where he often enjoyed the hospitality of his wealthy friend Walter Morrison, and discovered not only the setting for *The Water Babies*, but an epitome of the North itself . . .

'For the bottom of the valley was just one field broad, and on the other side ran the stream and above it, grey crag, grey down, grey stair, grey moor, walled up to heaven . . . Vendale . . . such a country, and such a people, as ought to make you proud of being a British boy.'

The appeal to patriotism in a fairy story, albeit a Victorian classic, reads 'preachy' today, but what does clearly emerge is Kingsley's sincere excitement awakened by the hidden peace and beauty of a dale which seems now to have changed little since his time. Of course you will see a tractor today, stabled in an old barn: Kingsley never saw a tractor. But he could very likely have seen the barn, for buildings here bear dates that show them to have been built long before he was born.

This deep U-shaped valley, patterned with mortar-free limestone walls, offers a perfect illustration of the classic dale formation. Unlike so much of Wharfedale, Littondale was never the scene of leadmining. The Forest of Litton was set aside by England's Norman conquerors to be a hunting ground, subject, like the Forest of Langstrothdale, to special laws. Here, until six hundred years ago, roamed the wild boar, and the deer – while wolves survived long enough to plague the monks who grazed their sheep here.

Hawkswick, the first village in the dale, nests on the northern side of the Skirfare. Was this neat hamlet named after a Viking warrior (the suffix *wick* means village), or after hawks which nested on the steep fells? Since Arncliffe, the next village up the dale, bears a name meaning Eagle's Rock, I choose the latter version, though the nearest thing to an eagle that you are likely to see today in these Pennine dales, barring the occasional vagrant, is the buzzard. But that is no mean substitute for an eagle, and I would welcome the sight of one against the green, towering walls of 'Amerdale'.

Hawkswick bears clear traces of its antiquity in the form of 'lynchets', the terraces made on the fell sides by Anglian farmers to enable their ploughing oxen (usually eight, yoked two abreast) to keep their feet on the steeply sloping ground. Littondale abounds in pathways and one to Arncliffe follows the riverside through fields of buttercups beside ancient trees.

It was too much to hope that Arncliffe would stay undiscovered by the modern world, epitomized by television. Hence it became, for a time, the village backcloth for *Emmerdale Farm*; 'a soap opera', if you like, but one which makes a commendable effort at presenting dales folk in credible form. But why was it thought necessary to change the name of the village inn from The Falcon (another bird of prey, you notice) to The Woolpack? Were they over-anxious to introduce the popular image of Yorkshire as a 'woollen' sort of county?

Beside the river, spanned here by a three-arched bridge, St Oswald's Church has a mid-fifteenth-century tower. The rest of the church was rebuilt in 1841. Critics may complain of its 'churchwarden Gothic' style, while the voluble Dr Whitaker called it 'a plain, oblong, ill-constructed building without aisles, choir, columns, battlement or buttress', with 'roof and wainscotting of deal; the covering of slate'. But I like its simplicity, and despite the rebuilding it breathes antiquity. A display case on the west wall contains a chalice dated 1619, a paten dated 1693 and an eighteenth-century silver cup. A halberd hangs on the wall near a list of Littondale men who fought at Flodden in 1513.

Cross the bridge from the church and you reach Bridge End, the house visited by Charles Kingsley from Malham Tarn House. One day he had walked over from Malham by the path still marked and much used today. Miss Elizabeth Hammond, who lived at Bridge House, offered him tea and thus stepped inadvertently into literature, for Kingsley put her in his fairy tale as 'the lady with a red petticoat'. On his way back to Malham, so the story goes, he sat on a favourite rock by the riverside and smoked one of his much-loved pipes; for in those days, when tobacco was often considered virtually medicinal, even the high priest of muscular Christianity could enjoy the weed with a good conscience.

Arncliffe, at least as I recall it now, would gain few prizes for primness; its green is divided up by a road which wanders about, pausing in front of the ancient pump but opting, instead, to pay a call at the Falcon Inn. Clover, buttercups and cow parsley were rife on the green, creating the impression of a village lost in a deep green sleep, whose few visitors moved about its 'stone-slated' cottages like people in a dream. A barn bears a datestone of 1677 and a house announces silently that it was built in 1730 – by MTE. Behind the barns and houses, small fields divided by drystone walls of limestone climb the sheltering slopes towards the moorland.

Just up-dale on the road which runs north of the river is Old Cote, a seventeenth-century yeoman's house which gives its name to many of its surrounding features – Old Cote Moor, Old Cote Low Moor, Old Cote Little Moor, Old Cote High Moor. This lovely dwelling with its projecting porch and staircase turret on the left between porth and house, epitomizes the unhurried past life of Littondale, where men had time to think and to build into their houses such enduring strength and grace.

Arncliffe seems a city compared with Litton, two miles up the dale. Here a line of grey cottages and farm buildings, a guest house and an inn, The Queen's Arms, seems to shelter in the fold of a giant palm. The only noise comes from the chattering Skirfare crossed by a narrow wooden bridge affording views of the 'Bright Stream' as it roars over miniature cataracts.

Another two miles up-dale brings you to Halton Gill, where a notice on Church House tells you it was 'formerly the Church of St John the Baptist'. And not just the church, for this long, low building with its bell cote still in place, was church and school combined, as well as home to the curate, Miles Wilson, who served both as parson and schoolmaster, teaching downstairs in the schoolroom and living above.

Less than a mile brings you to Foxup, a hamlet indeed. It lends its name to Foxup Beck, which, with its companion Cosh Beck, gives birth to the Skirfare. Beyond Foxup there is only Cosh, the farthest outpost of Littondale and long known as Yorkshire's loneliest farmhouse.

Back in main-line Wharfedale, I found Kettlewell's church, St Mary's, open – and rejoiced. So many churches in these benighted days offer no sanctuary on weekdays either to the devout or the curious. Understandable, but a pity, for there are few better places to begin a village exploration than the parish church, especially one founded as long ago as this – in the reign of Henry I, say the records.

The original St Mary's, built in Norman times, was largely replaced last century, except for the tower. But through all the changing scenes of ecclesiastical life an ornamental early Norman or late Saxon tub front has given baptism to countless generations of infant dalesmen and their women since the first recorded incumbent, 'Raduldhus, decanus de Ketelwella', was appointed to his post by the Abbot of Coverham.

Ancient and modern entwine themselves at every turn in Kettlewell. In the church porch a notice warns that 'there are in the surrounding pastures and moorland, disused mine shafts which should not be approached as they may prove dangerous.' It is signed 'The Manor of Kettlewell'.

Such manors, usually governed by Trust Lords elected from the Freeholders, represent a form of village government which is little understood outside the Pennines. These worthies, sometimes known as Wise Men, have all the functions and powers of Lords of the Manor, holding their lordship in trust for all the freeholders of the township. Many of the groups date from the late sixteenth century and each has its own peculiar constitution. They originated after the Dissolution of the Monasteries, when great areas of the Dales, formerly used for sheep farming, were returned to the Crown and eventually sold to local lords or families. More land went to the Crown after the Rising of the North in 1569, when staunch northern Catholics, including such great families as the Nevilles and the Percies, tried to restore Catholicism and secure the succession of Mary Queen of Scots.

The defeat of the Rising meant that lands formerly owned by the rebels were sequestered and often sold to London merchants, who resold them to local purchasers, though many remained the property of the Crown and were frequently mismanaged through being so far away from central control. During the reigns of James I and Charles I, when ready money was sought to redevelop the Navy, much of this Crown land was sold via London merchants to local individuals or groups on trust for all the manorial tenants. Thus arose the Trust Lords of the Dales.

Kettlewell is said to derive its name from an Irish-Norse chieftain who had a well here. It is a pleasant jumble of a place filled with all the evidence of active village life. Throughout its long history, certainly since the thirteenth century when a market was established, it has thrived, for textiles were manufactured here before the lead-mining boom of the eighteenth and early nineteenth centuries. Half a mile above the village, close to where the Cam and Dawber Becks converge, are the remains of a smelting mill dating from 1700 and in use up to a century ago.

But Kettlewell's future, like it or not, lies with the tourists. It has three popular inns. The Racehorses, the Blue Bell and the King's Head, besides holiday cottages and guest houses so numerous that the place almost seems to belong to the visitors.

Kettlewell offers two routes up-dale to Wensleydale, both dotted with villages, yet differing subtly in character. The easterly road, the minor of the two, climbs by way of the notorious Park Rash (in places 1 in 4) to Coverdale, one of the delectable 'little dales' which hide themselves away from the mainstream. But exploration of Coverdale can be postponed until we reach its northern ends, at Middleham or Wensley.

First we come to Starbotton, with its rather magical (if oft mispronounced) name, a jumble of buildings not unlike the probable result if a toy-bricked village were upset and hastily reassembled. The reason: in 1686 Wharfedale's worst ever flood wiped out all but a few of the houses then standing in the village. When order was restored and rebuilding began with the aid of Sunday collections donated from all over England, the results were hasty and somewhat haphazard, though possessing a charm that might otherwise have been absent.

Buckden (population 200) has a long history of local music-making and folk dancing. It seems a pity therefore (or am I being unrealistic?) that Buckden folk should have seen it as a crisis when they were faced with the loss of their TV programmes due to the 'phasing out' of 405-line transmission and its replacement by the 625-line system.

The very hills which once made Buckden a self-contained world of Dales culture were now in danger of isolating it from TV advertising and American soap operas. But let no-one say dales folk are unequal to such technological threats. Promptly, those affected by the change-over formed the Buckden Cable TV group to run their own reception booster equipment. Aided by the Yorkshire Rural Community Council, they drew up plans to receive signals from Kettlewell's transmitter by way of a master aerial in the village, relayed by cable to their homes, the site of the aerial being the property of the West Yorkshire Police Authority. The equipment they needed would cost £4000, half of which they raised themselves, the Development Commission funding the other half. It was the first grant of its kind made from the Commission's HQ in distant London under a new scheme to help just such groups who have viewing problems in remote country areas. Now each household in the scheme pays £10 a year towards operational and maintenance costs.

At the foot of the 2302-foot Buckden Pike, the village is rarely without visitors, at least during the spring and summer, who stop off on their journey higher into the Dales for a drink or a snack or to use the convenient public lavatories while their cars cool their engines in the car park. But in past days the village was far busier. Here resided the guardians of Langstrothdale Chase, where deer were hunted – the 'bucks' which gave Buckden its name, and the Buck Inn too, of course. In those days it was one of the three inns thronged with farmers and the merchants who came here to buy wool from the sheep pastured on these fells.

I, for one, reject Buckden's 'last village in Wharfedale' claim, for Langstrothdale, which strikes westward to join Wensleydale, is surely in the Wharfe Valley, is indeed the river's birthplace; and in Langstrothdale we have Hubberholme, as no-one knew better than Miles Wilson...

Miles, a curate as you may recall at Halton Gill at the end of Littondale, must often have studied the winter slopes with foreboding some two and a half centuries ago, for it was his additional responsibility to serve the chapel of ease at Hubberholme. Ruefully, he records the difficulty and danger of passing over 'very high mountains' and fighting his way through large drifts of snow to reach the chapel. I get the feeling, perhaps unjust to Miles's memory, that he found it an onerous extra duty to serve the one-time little forest chapel, built, at first, on a burial site once used by the Anglo-Norse settlers. Paradoxically, this peaceful hamlet takes its name from the belligerent Viking Hubba, who found the wild dales to his liking and settled here.

The chapel was certainly here in 1241, for that was the year William de Percy gave it to the monks of Coverham Abbey. It included, then, a chamber and a garden for a priest, whose duty required him to pray for the souls of the de Percys. Doubtless, when the clouds over Langstrothdale betokened snow, Miles Wilson wished that a resident priest prayed for them still.

Hubberholme church is worth visiting, if only for its rood loft, dated 1558, and bearing the name William Jake. How did this delicate piece of work, carved in the reign of Mary Tudor, survive the austere 'reforms' of Protestant rule? Did it ever accommodate the musicians for which it was no doubt intended? Probably the remoteness of Hubberholme in medieval times preserved the usages of the old religion when they were swept away elsewhere. Today this rare and lovely gallery is a treasured fixture and William Jake, wherever he is, can rejoice that his masterpiece is as safe as the 'mice', trademark of another Yorkshire village craftsman, Bob Thompson of Kilburn, which hide among the pews, chairs and choir stalls.

So close is the Wharfe to the squat Norman building, with its stump of a tower, that in times of flood, fish – trout, surely – have swum in the nave providing, one hopes, some tasty manna for the vicar. Across the hump-backed bridge is the George Inn, where once the vicar could have taken his fish to fry: for in bygone days it was the vicarage. At least once a year that reverend sir may still be seen in the George – all very properly – for on the first Monday of January he is quite likely to auction the 'Poor Pasture' there for charity. This land, six hectares, or 16 acres, left in trust to the village for the needy, goes to the highest bidder among the farmers, the 'Commons' who, sitting in the bar, form part of this truly ancient 'Parliament'. The vicar and church wardens, whose place is the parlour, represent the 'Lords', while the 'needy' of today are the village pensioners. These convivial proceedings follow lunch provided by the landlord.

Beyond Hubberholme, the hamlets of Yockenthwaite and Oughtershaw survive from the days when they too were founded by Norse settlers, to serve later as sites of Norman forest lodges. As the Wharfe becomes little more than a stream, swirling and eddying over the limestone beds, the wildness increases. And above Yockenthwaite a lonely Bronze Age stone circle makes even the most venerable village seem a newcomer.

Nun Monkton, at the point where the Nidd joins the Ouse, appears to take life easily, if not frivolously. Its inn, the Alice Hawthorn, is named after a race-horse: it is presumably as tolerant and solicitous of human frailty as it is of the numerous ducks that populate the pond on the green, where a maypole adds a further hedonistic hint.

Nun Monkton's name was originally Monechtone, being named, they say, from a hermit, whose cell stood on the site now occupied by the lovely church of St Mary, which, with a modesty appropriate to a nunnery, seems to hide behind a weeping beech tree. After all, its original purpose was to serve as chapel to a community of Benedictine sisters, founded here in the twelfth century.

The hermit's cell was destroyed by raiding Vikings and later by vengeful Normans, when the villagers defied the Conqueror (for Nun Monkton was not always so peaceful as it now appears). When the fury had abated, William de Arches, a descendant of Osbern de Arches, who had 'pacified' this village given him by the Bastard, had qualms of conscience on his own or his ancestor's account and in 1158 founded the priory to atone for the family's sins. He installed his daughter, Matilda, as prioress and nearly four centuries later it was her successor, Joanna Slingsby, who handed the priory to Henry VIII.

At Moor Monkton across the river, Charles I slept at Red House (now a school). Further south, scattered around Marston Moor (where an obelisk commemorates Cromwell's victory over that unlucky monarch) are Hessay, Rufforth, Long Marston and Tockwith. Cowthorpe, where Guy Fawkes rang the church bells as a boy, may still cherish the corpse of its 'thousand-year-old' oak, but not for long, I fear.

A mile or two to the south-west, Spofforth has a sturdy Norman Revival-style church containing the effigy of a fourteenth-century local knight, Robert Plumpton, some worthy and hospitable pubs, and the remains of the castle where Harry Hotspur was born.

Search the churchyard and you will find the grave of one of the most remarkable Yorkshiremen who ever trod the Broad Acres. And certainly few trod them to greater effect. I refer to John Metcalf, Blind Jack of Knaresborough, who, despite the loss of his sight when he was only six years old, led an amazing life as forest guide, fiddler and even soldier (during the Forty-Five Rebellion). He snatched the girl of his choice from under her parents' noses on the night before she was to have been married to the man of *their* choice – though certainly not of hers.

But Jack's greatest claim to fame is as a maker of roads. He built nearly 200 miles of them – often in places where others had tried and failed. To tell his whole story would require a book, but his gravestone in Spofforth churchyard bears an excellent summary in rhyming couplets –

> *'Twas his a guide's unerring aid to lend;*
> *O'er trackless wastes to bid new roads extend . . .*

Jack retired to Spofforth, where he died in 1810 in his ninety-third year. His funeral may well have been conducted by John Tripp, who was rector from 1783 to 1814 (and, incidentally, great-great-great-great-grandfather of Princess Anne's husband, Mark Phillips). Many of Spofforth's rectors were notable in their own time. There was Matthew Hutton, later Archbishop of York and of Canterbury, and the Hon. William Herbert, barrister and a Member of Parliament, scholar and botanist, pursuing his studies in the garden of his rectory. A variety of crocus, Herbertia of Sweet, was named after him.

From Spofforth a minor road leads north-eastwards to Ribston, where the seventeenth-century Ribston Hall, home of the famous Ribston pippin, has been virtually reborn.

The house was built in 1674 by Sir Henry Goodricke and 'Georgianized' around 1780, probably by John Carr of York. Living arrangements in the venerable pile had hardly changed since the 1890s. Then in 1978 Charles Dent, a chartered surveyor, inherited the house on the banks of the Nidd from his grandfather, Geoffrey Dent, who, with his wife in their later years, had shared with their old retainers a faithful concern for the house and the standards it had enshrined. Since Howard, the butler, was mistrustful of electricity, he kept oil lamps trimmed as he had done for half a century.

In the late seventies all three – owners and butler – died within a few years of each other. Then in 1980 the new owners began a five-year process of restoration, first demolishing the nineteenth-century service extension, the materials from which were either sold or used to restore the main building. Today the house is at least as habitable and certainly as cherished as in the days when Sir Henry Goodricke, 4th Bart., lived here and raised the Ribston Pippin from seeds introduced into England from Normandy in 1705. The ancestor of the Cox's orange pippin, it lived, much cossetted, until 1835 and now its descendants still stand among new specimens introduced by the present owner.

Dating from Norman times, the estate was at one time owned by the Knights Templar and the Knights of St John of Jerusalem, but its most famous owner was the second baronet, Sir Henry Goodricke, a supporter of William of Orange in 1688. On the medieval chapel of the Knights Templar, now the parish church of Great Ribston, a tablet of 1703 records its 'refurbishment and embellishment' by Sir Henry 'in the 12th year of King William, our deliverer from Popery and slavery'.

North of here is Goldsborough, whose hall was the first Yorkshire home of the Princess Royal, while to the west at Follifoot stands Rudding Park. A name identified with this fine Regency house is perpetuated by the sign of the Radcliffe Arms, while another illustrious title is borne by its companion, the Lascelles Arms.

There is no hint of whimsicality in the choice of stocks as a memorial to two no doubt blameless village notables; Amy Winifred Robinson, of Priory Lodge, and Colonel Gerard Maxwell Glynton, D.S.O., of The Priory. At all events, the stocks were restored to their memory in 1957 and given a neat roof (which was surely a benefit never enjoyed by the original occupants). Also well preserved here is the village pinfold, where straying beasts were once impounded.

Minutes of a Parish Council meeting on public display told me that according to the 1981 census, Follifoot contained 177 households, 128 of which were those of owner-occupiers; there were 480 residents, 223 male and 257 female. The village boasted (or admitted to) 240 cars, ridden in or driven by a population divided by age as follows: Under 15, 93; 15–64, 281; 65–74, 83; 75-plus, 32. Less recent but more poignant statistics were those in the little war memorial shelter – 18 killed in 1914–18 and seven in 1939–45.

But Follifoot today is a cheerful place with gay umbrellas outside the pubs on sunny days and everywhere a proper pride in the charm which in 1980 won it a seat inscribed 'Best kept village in the Lower Dales'.

Villages too numerous even to list surround Harrogate and Knaresborough. Off the Ripon Road to the east is the hamlet of Nidd whose name is shared with both river and dale. North of the river, at the western side of that same road (A61), Ripley Castle reigns over one of the most remarkable villages in Yorkshire. But if this is really Yorkshire, why is the village hall inscribed 'Hotel de Ville'. Surprising? But then this village has had more than a touch of the fairy tale about it from the day 700 years ago when Thomas Ingilby saved King Edward III from a charging boar in Knaresborough Forest and was rewarded with this same estate.

The romantic Ingilbys still live at Ripley and a colourful lot they have been. Take Sir William, who sided with Guy Fawkes and was only saved from the block by bribing the chief prosecution witnesses to change their evidence. Or the Lady Ingilby who, as the best known family tale relates, tucked pistols in her apron and stayed awake all night watching Oliver Cromwell, an unwelcome 'guest' after the Battle of Marston Moor, as he passed an uneasy night on the sofa. Her husband Sir William was away fighting the Roundheads at the time, with his sister, Trooper Jane, who dressed, fought and perhaps cursed like any other soldier.

It was Sir William Amcotts Ingilby who in 1827 transformed the village with its thatched cottages into his conception of an Alsatian village, though beyond referring to his castle as 'the schloss' he was presumably content to leave it in its Tudor style. The cobbled square, market cross and stocks, too, remind you that this was a village long before the eighteenth century.

Nor could Sir William do much to change All Saints' Church, whose walls bear the marks of Roundhead bullets. That church replaced one which stood on a hill which subsided into the River Nidd nearly six centuries ago. History may almost be repeating itself, for in December 1985 the Historic Buildings Commission reported that part of the castle was sinking into the waterlogged sand on which it stood, and needed urgent and costly repairs if it were to survive.

Ironically, the oldest parts of the building are not at risk, but the eighteenth-century extensions, which are said to have been poorly designed and possibly built in a hurry because the wife of the then incumbent, John (1757–1815), was expecting to come into a large fortune. The present state of the building would no doubt have given grim satisfaction to Cromwell, who scrawled a warning against 'pompe and pride' beneath a laudatory Ingilby memorial in the church.

'Pompe' is not so noticeable now among the Ingilbys: a recent press photograph of the present owner, Sir Thomas, in his early thirties, shows him sitting casually on a farm fence as he discusses his plans to please the tourists and expresses his impatience with glass cases and barriers. But pride they have in plenty, not least of one early Ingilby who may have been declared a saint by the time this book appears. A Roman Catholic priest, he was hanged, drawn and quartered on the Knavesmire, where now York races are run. The priest-hole, where he may have hidden, in the wainscoting of the Knight's Chamber at the top of the tower, was only discovered in 1963; yet even such secret hiding places were clearly not secure enough to ensure his safety.

Since Sir William Amcotts Ingilby completed his transformation of the village over 150 years ago, there had been no significant new development in the village until a terrace of five new cottages was completed in 1986 and offered at prices ranging from £45 950 to £49 000.

South-west of Ripley, Hampsthwaite offeres a surprising variety of celebrities. In its church of St Thomas à Becket lies the white marble effigy of Amy Woodforde-Finden, composer of the Indian Love Lyrics. The village was also the home of the locally famous 'Blind Peter' Barker, almost as great a prodigy in his triumph over sightlessness as

Blind Jack of Knaresborough. Peter's tombstone in the graveyard
records his skill as 'cabinet maker, glazier and musician'. But perhaps
the most surprising resident of this peaceful graveyard is William
Makepeace Thackeray, whose family had lived here for generations.
The tiny cottage where he used to stay while visiting his relatives still
stands outside the village.

Almost due north of Hampsthwaite there is Bedlam (whose
inhabitants must surely be inured to some leg-pulling) with, nearby,
Burnt Yates, Summerbridge and – would you believe? – New York.

South of here, at Darley, the seventeenth-century water-powered
corn mill beside Darley Beck has been restored in the interests of
tourists. When they are tired of admiring the 27-feet diameter pitch
shot water wheel, they may spend money on linen in the mills store
room or on 'crafts and gifts' in the erstwhile grain store. Then refresh
themselves on traditional Yorkshire 'fayre' at a restaurant and tea shop
in the old miller's cottage. Traditionalists may bemoan such transfor-
mations (not to mention the 'olde worlde' spelling) but surely this is
better than the all-too-frequent alternative – crumbling ruins inhabited
by the ghosts of melancholy.

At Dacre Banks, near Summerbridge, mining monks of Fountains
Abbey had a grange. Low Laithe and Wilsill are close to Brimham
Rocks, which attract thousands of visitors to marvel at the rock
formations whose shapes are hardly more grotesque than some of the
names bestowed on them – appellations as varied as The Druid's Coffin
and Donald Duck.

Should you journey this way from Grassington in Wharfedale, you
will pass through Greenhow Hill and see Nidderdale at its bleakest . . .
'It's a wild old place, all right,' said one of the two Americans in the bar
of the Miner's Arms at Greenhow. I wondered what had brought them
to this ghost of a miner's village. The pit lamps that hang above the
landlord's head as he pulls his pints were once carried far beneath the
undulating surface of Greenhow, at the foot of whose hill lies Pateley
Bridge. As you descend that hill, increasingly frantic road signs warn
you to proceed in low gear and remind you of hair-raising gradients.

In the Miner's Arms the talk was still of the lead-miners who long ago
vanished from the bleak and chilling scene. In memory they are as
much alive as the gold-miners of the Old West in the homeland of those
visiting Americans, now drinking rum and ginger ale. It was July, but
under a lowering sky the wind was cold. Photographs on the walls, of
gaunt, bearded, cheerless looking men at the sites of their back-
breaking toil were hardly conducive to jollity.

Few Yorkshire villages – which surely means few in England – are
higher than Greenhow, more than 1300 feet above sea level: if, indeed,
this can be called a village. For there is little here besides a pub and a

church, said to be the second highest parish church in England.

Set apart from the church at the crest of a hill is the loneliest graveyard in England. A lych-gate gives entrance and you pass beneath the inscription *I will lift up mine eyes to the hills from whence cometh my help*. Slightly inaccurate, for here you seem to be looking down from the hills.

A roadside war memorial, embellished with a hammer, lists 'Greenhow men and women' who died in the First World War. Their total seems to outnumber by far any possible present-day population of this short-lived village, born in the early seventeenth century for the sole purpose of lead mining. The industry reached its peak in the eighteenth and nineteenth centuries and was already in decline when the cemetery was consecrated in 1895 by the Bishop of Ripon and the war memorial with its hammer emblem was unveiled.

Today every second scattered building, including one labelled in wrought iron 'The Old School House', seems to be For Sale. The toilers of the past would doubtless marvel that the scene of their labours and the cottages where they lived should be sought after by holidaymakers of a later century.

Before the Romans came, lead with a good silver-rich content was mined at Greenhow. In the eighteenth century two pigs of lead were discovered here bearing a first-century Roman inscription. One is preserved in the British Museum and one in Ripley Castle. In later times the monks of Fountains Abbey smelted the lead to roof the abbey, and the monastery grew rich on the metal brought from workings far beneath the moors.

Where now the cars of bemused, half-fearful tourists squeeze through the narrow lanes, sure-footed pack horses bore away the metal hewn at their peril by men whose toil took them from the light of day.

One day in 1858 the search for lead took two miners a mile or two to the west of Greenhow, into a realm which made them doubt what the light from their flickering lamps revealed. They had stumbled into Stump Cross Caverns, one of the 'show caves' of the Dales where the wonders of stalactite and stalagmite are now revealed by powerful lights.

Though lead-mining ceased nearly a century ago after a severe drop in lead prices in the 1860s, the miners survive in story and in the ghost of 'T'Owd Man', who persists in making his spectral presence felt or heard. More prosaic successors of the indomitable tunnellers who left their harsh subterranean world to face one almost equally harsh above ground, where winter came early and lingered late, are the stone quarrymen and fluorspar recoverers.

Pateley Bridge, at the foot of Greenhow Hill, is a veritable metropolis compared with Greenhow. But is it a village? I would say no, though it recently came first in the 'Large Village' class of the Beautiful Britain in Bloom competition. Perhaps it is the sombreness of the millstone grit of which Pateley is largely built, and that tunnel-like main street where tall houses and shops conspire to exclude the sunlight, that inspires folk here to brighten their town, village, what you will, with flowers wherever flowers can be grown.

Not everyone approves of the floral Pateley. To some it seems out of keeping with its sober history of lead mining, reservoir and railway building that it should now cavort, as one reporter put it, like a schoolmarm dressed up in a can-can dress. The Nidderdale town, said the same observer, 'with the solid dark grey buildings, is turning itself into something resembling a Swiss or Black Forest village . . . a riot of flowers all summer long.'

Despite its 2500 inhabitants, its magistrates' court, its theatre and magnificent do-it-yourself museum, Pateley ('the field of the badger') may be technically a town, but it has the heart of a village, cherishing memories of folk heroes like Jack Sinclair, the poacher, and Lish (Elisha), his brother. Jack's powder flask now rests in the museum to which it was proudly presented by one of his descendants, full of stories she first heard from her grandmother who took food to Jack while he hid from the police for five days in a drain pipe. Jack and Lish, true inheritors of the Robin Hood tradition, were the talk of Pateley for their generosity and daring. Many a poor old woman opened her front door to find a poached rabbit lying there, courtesy of the brothers Sinclair. Their life was a continual game of hide and seek with the police, to which spice was added by the brothers' habit of disguising themselves in women's clothing. The townsfolk were invariably on the side of the brothers, tearing down 'wanted' posters and giving them whatever aid they could. But even the best games have to end, and in those days the scales were more heavily weighted on the side of law and order than on daring and generosity. After his trial at York Assizes, poor Lish was transported to Van Diemen's land, much mourned by the folk of Nidderdale.

The museum that houses Jack's powder flask is a relic in its own right. Built in 1860 as a workhouse, its 'unsettled poor' were moved out in 1914 to make room for prisoners of war. It reverted to its original function between the wars, then, in 1939, became the council offices. In 1974 it found an immensely valuable rôle as the repository for a marvellous collection of Niddersdale bygones. Here is the recreated cobbler's shop of the Binks family, whose handmade shoes and boots were sold in the Dales by three generations of Binkses, each called Christopher. By packhorse track they travelled, mostly on foot, though the last Christopher was the proud owner of a bicycle.

Pateley, constituted a market town as long ago as the fourteenth century and still the setting for a fortnightly sheep and cattle market, bears few traces of its medieval origins. High above the town, the church of St Mary, which dates from the mid-thirteenth century, is a roofless ruin. The present church, built in 1827, stands in King Street along with the workhouse and the gaol-like school building with its sharp pointed tower, all revealing this to be essentially a Victorian town developed by, though certainly not born of, the industrial age.

Lead and iron, mined here for centuries, were even more in demand as the machine age turned the West Riding into one of the great workshops of the world. As industry swelled the population of the Riding, stone was needed for houses and Nidderdale's quarries expanded to meet the demand.

In 1862 the North Eastern Railway opened a branch line from Harrogate to Pateley Bridge. They renamed it 'Little Switzerland' and the tourists flocked here by the thousand from the dark streets and smoky air of the mill towns such as Bradford, for whose thirsty mills and workers, the River Nidd was imprisoned in three great man-made lakes in the lonely upper reaches of the dale. To carry workers to these haunts of curlew and lapwing, the single-line Nidd Valley Light Railway was opened in 1907, Britain's first municipally owned railway with stations at Wath, Ramsgill and Lofthouse. You can still trace the route followed by the track, though the rails were taken up 50 years after the more efficient and economic motor buses had taken over.

Much of the history of the reservoirs and their builders can be gleaned in the museum, where reservoir building workers were once billeted until a new 'village' was erected for them in the higher reaches of the dale. Now nothing remains of it but traces of where the buildings stood.

Such events – mining, the railway and reservoir building – periodically brought badly needed prosperity to what was regarded in the leaner times between as 'the forgotten dale'. Monuments to those hard times are the remains of the 'stoop' called 'Yorke's Folly', which was one of three erected by the Yorke family during a period of low employment.

Travelling up Nidderdale your eyes are constantly tempted to wander to Gouthwaite, on the right, where the Nidd widens into a man-made reservoir that surely deserves to be called a lake. It is in fact the site of a glacial lake. Whether the birds appreciate its beauties or not they have certainly flocked here in great variety – two hundred species of them, from dippers to golden eagles have found this two-mile stretch of water an irresistible haven. Beneath its shimmering surface lies the old house of the Yorkes.

The more Gouthwaite lures our eyes to its spacious glitter and its tenants of varied plumage, the more Ramsgill takes us by surprise as we find ourselves suddenly enclosed by its delightful grouping of church and inn and village hall with mullioned windows, around a green which the road crosses by two bridges, over sparkling waters bordered by ferns and shaded by venerable horse chestnuts and copper beeches.

We should not be *too* surprised to find ourselves in this magical miniature of a village; the tower of St Mary the Virgin would have warned us if we had not been so absorbed by the charms of Gouthwaite. Outside the Yorke Arms (once the family's shooting lodge) on a sign picked out in fairy lights which, touched by the prevailing magic, lack any taint of vulgarity, are displayed the arms of the Yorke family.

It will not take long to explore the church, a simple and modest little edifice dating only from 1842, though even here there are surprises, like the small gable, the only surviving relic of the original chapelry, built into the wall of the churchyard. Were the monks of Byland Abbey who built that chapelry the first inhabitants of Ramsgill? They had a grange hereabouts in 1143, from which grew a small, industrious lay settlement with a corn mill powered by the tumbling Ramsgill Beck.

The village hall, so agreeable a sight after some of the eyesores desecrating the Dales, was converted from a stone barn and shows it very agreeably in contrast with the pebble dash examples seen not far away. It could hardly be more integral to the village, incorporating, as it does, a link with the village's famous – or infamous – son, Eugene Aram; for the strange round carved face set in an outside wall of the hall is said to be a portrait of Aram's mother, though it may be Roman or even earlier in origin.

Eugene Aram's story survives not least because of its truly tragic element. He was a strange, brilliant creature, who fell into bad company and was hanged for murder when a skeleton was discovered 13 years after his alleged crime.

Apart from such gruesome reflections, Ramsgill is a place where every prospect pleases. This is a heavenly place for walkers, as probably Eugene discovered; though on one of the loveliest of those walks, along the riverside to Lofthouse a couple of miles up-dale, his eyes were no doubt less dazzled by the beauty of the scenery than by his companion, Anna Spence, who became his partner in a disastrous marriage.

Despite its closeness to Ramsgill, Lofthouse is a quirkier, less gentle-looking village. Its climbing, twisting street is lined with sturdy stone cottages (many of them now holiday homes), some with tiny gardens and some combined with what were once cowsheds above which was a hayloft reached by a flight of stone steps up the front of the house. An endowed school founded in the eighteenth century for 'ten poor boys' still caters for a handful of pupils. The village grew around a grange established by the monks of Fountains Abbey and in 1251, monks of

Byland Abbey mined ironstone by means of bell pits, so named because of their narrow openings which widened into a 'bell' shape.

In the middle of the Crown Hotel car park grows a tree planted in 1977 to mark the fiftieth anniversary of Lofthouse village hall, a source of considerable village pride and serving a worthy purpose in the multifarious activities of village life reflected in the notice board nearby. It advertised a steam engine rally at Masham in Wensleydale, a dozen miles or so distant by way of Colsterdale and a road that not long ago was unfit for motor vehicles. A gate at this end of the village seems to wait to be closed should Lofthouse feel the outside world is pressing too close upon it.

The little war memorial cross seems to share the quirky air of the village where Anna Spence, Eugene Aram's wife, first saw the light. Its doggerel verses in praise of 'cold water inside and out' is signed JR, initials believed to be those of a Scotsman, John Rayner – probably hounded from his native heath because of his views on the benefits of *aqua pura*! But it is also claimed that a stonemason called Drummond left the memorial fountain as a memento of the time he spent in Lofthouse working on the reservoir dams.

There is plenty of water at How Stean close by, where a wooded gorge 70 or 80 feet deep has been worn over countless ages by what is now the How Stean Beck. Rustic bridges cross and recross the chasm and for a small charge – so may you.

I love the bleakness of Middlesmoor, the last village in the dale. Its first church was consecrated in 1484 by the Archbishop of York, in response to pleas from villagers whose mother church had until then been at Kirkby Malzeard in Wensleydale. The present church dates only from 1866, but it holds treasures much older, like a part of a cross to St Chad, who preached here in 664, and an ancient bell.

Eugene Aram climbed to a church here in 1731 with Anna Spence to marry and leave their signatures in the register. There were probably even fewer cottages then and surely no Methodist chapel to nod at you on the one-in-four gradient road which takes you to the very roof of Nidderdale.

Middlesmoor marks the head of the dale, beyond which there is only moorland and mountain and more reservoirs. Yet to the south of the great whale-shaped Scar House Reservoir the grass retains the impress of that village specially built for workmen and their families, and once populated by 1250 souls.

4

By Ure and Swale

FISHERMEN AND HORNBLOWERS

In the base of the churchyard wall at Wath, may be found a carved Saxon stone, at which village girls used to 'christen' their dolls. For Wath is an ancient place. The Domesday Book records that the 'vill', with its church, was given by William the Conqueror to Alan, Earl of Brittany. The foundations of that pre-Conquest church, which stood on the site of the present one, were discovered during the restoration of St Mary's Church in 1873, along with a number of other Saxon stones, three of which have been built into the wall of the choir vestry.

Less than a mile from the village is Norton Conyers, the original of Thornfield, the house of Rochester in Charlotte Brontë's *Jane Eyre*. The great Hall of this fine Jacobean mansion has given hospitality to many monarchs. The estate belonged to the Norton family until they had to surrender it to the crown on the attainder of Richard Norton for his part in the Rising of the North. Sir Richard Musgrave bought it from the crown in 1593 and in 1624 Musgrave's eldest son sold it to Sir Richard Graham, whose family still owns it.

A walled garden dating from the eighteenth century is still under cultivation, while inside the house there is a wealth of paintings, costumes and manuscripts, besides a Brontë collection.

Village churchyards have surprising tenants. Hiding among flaking Georgian tombstones at West Tanfield a few miles up the dale, are the graves of two authors of what many would salute as modern minor classics. Certainly *Grayling and How to Catch Them*, first published in 1895, is a classic to discerning Yorkshire anglers. It was written by Francis Walbran, who did much of his fishing on the West Tanfield reaches of the Ure and on one occasion covered seven miles of the river, wading every inch of the way. He rarely missed a day on the water if it were fishable at all, and finally paid for his passion with his life. On the stone cross that marks his resting place is recorded his accidental death by drowning in 1909. And carved beneath that inscription is a set of verses that ends, *The voice of the river shall sing to him still.*

Sleeping not far away is R.W.S. Bishop, who died on 31 December 1921. His book, *My Moorland Patients* (since republished as *Moorland Doctor*), is one of the most closely-observed accounts of moorland dwellers in south and north-west Yorkshire. He died shortly before his book was published, going to rest beneath his modest stone convinced that his anonymous authorship would never be discovered; that he would be remembered only as a country doctor who spent his last few years at Tanfield. However, his death and notices of him which appeared in the newspapers were somehow considered to have 'removed this objection to giving his name as the author'. I hope this unsought acclaim does not disturb the peace of a truly beloved physician.

Other voices than the river's must surely speak in the dreams of Dr Bishop, and they will use the language he mastered to be sure his moorland patients could understand him. For he must often have been greeted at a bedside by the sort of complaint he quotes in his book: 'Ah's bad, Ah can tell yer. T'pain's past bahdin'. Mi shackles wark, mi belly warks, mi head warks, an' Ah warks all over ... Ah can eate nowt, an' Ah's that weeak an' wanklin, that yah moon mannish sharp er bottle er reight stuff te give mah gud mends, else it'll seean be owered wi' me.' (The which, being briefly translated means, 'I'm very ill and cannot bear the pain. I can eat nothing and am now so weak that unless you prescribe an efficacious remedy I shall soon die.')

So the Marmions, who lie in effigy inside St Nicholas's Church have neighbours outside with their own modest claim to fame. Most notable among the knightly sleepers within the church are Sir John Marmion and his lady, who rest in alabaster beneath an iron hearse, with prickets for candles, that is said to be unique in England.

Only the day before my visit an American had left a pencilled note near the church donations box saying, 'We have nothing like this in the U.S.A. nor would we dare leave our beautiful worship items in an open church. We do appreciate you English...' I hope the American visitors appreciated the whole of West Tanfield with its sleepy streets, where the only sound, beside the occasional car, was the somehow soothing whine of a power tool from a craft shop which turns out garden furniture.

Perhaps the Americans visited the Thornborough Circles, a mile or so from the church, or the Bronze Age barrows where earlier dalesfolk were buried. They would surely thrill to the Marmion Tower beside the church; it is all that remains of the castle that once stood here and which it served as gatehouse. You climb a spiral stone staircase to gain views of the river, sluggish in the summer heat between fields all too productive of tiny, tormenting harvest flies. Nobody could appreciate them.

A few miles south-west of Tanfield lies an area full of memories for me yet little known to the outside world. It centres on Kirkby Malzeard and its 'satellite' village, Grewelthorpe. On holiday long ago at the Queen's Head in Kirkby Malzeard, after breakfasting on trout fresh-caught in the Ure that morning by the ex-gamekeeper landlord, I would take the landlord's over-weight cocker spaniel on long walks from which, on at least one occasion, its unaccustomed muscles demanded a return by taxi.

In his later years Bing Crosby came annually for the grouse shooting and demonstrated his great affection for the place by his support of local charities.

Village folk are peaceable enough until they feel their rights are endangered. About four hundred years ago, Kirkby and Grewelthorpe, which are barely a mile apart, fell out over who had the right to dig for coal on Grewelthorpe Moor. Eventually an acceptable solution to the problem was found, but not before the women of the two villages had fought it out with spears and bows and arrows in a bloody conflict which resulted in some deaths.

Once Grewelthorpe was famous for its Wensleydale cheese but a more recent attraction has been a craft workshop producing hand-woven fine worsted cloth from a flock of the now fashionable four-horned Jacob sheep, which until recently could be fairly described as a 'rare' breed.

Masham (pronounced Massam) might scorn to be called a village but like many another Dales market town it has village qualities and is all the richer for that. Pause here to tour the town, with or without the aid of *A Walkabout Tour of Masham*, a leaflet published by Harrogate Resort Services Department. From the ancient market cross in the huge market place, the tour takes in the Grammar and Free Schools founded in 1760; the Old Poor House and its adjacent cell, used as a powder house in 1885 by the Masham Volunteers; the old mill house and the fine, tall-spired church with its pillar; part of a Saxon cross, and much else including College House, once the meeting place for the 'Peculier' Court. This ecclesiastical tribunal tried offenders for religious and moral crimes, punishing them sometimes by excommunication. A local brew of strong beer now bears the name Old Peculier, which would hardly have pleased the reverend gentlemen who sat in judgement on their more fallible fellows.

The little hillside village of Well marks the third point in a triangle it forms with West Tanfield and Masham. Its name denotes its original local purpose. For in the days when water was associated with divinity, here was a well at which the spirits were worshipped. And the presence of water here no doubt also accounts for the choice of Well as the site for a Roman official's villa. Parts of it were dug up in 1859, then, 70 years later, a portion of tessellated pavement was restored. For safety's sake it was taken into St Michael's Church and attached to the west wall of the nave.

Further evidence of Well's pagan past is the dedication of the church to the Archangel saint, for it was Michael's task to war upon the forces of evil, as the old gods were considered to be.

Sadly, Michael seems to have been ineffective against the Scots, who invaded the area more than six-and-a-half centuries ago and destroyed this and many other churches round here. The Norman doorway with its dogtooth carving is all that remains of what was probably the first stone church to replace the building mentioned in Domesday Book, but the font cover of 1352 may well be the second oldest in England.

Ralph Neville, who rebuilt the church, also endowed a hospital for 24 poor folk (12 men and 12 women), or 'cremets', as they were unflatteringly called, and in later centuries, in continuation of this charity, the Cecils erected the almhouses near the church.

A couple of miles north, towards Bedale, Snape is a village whose present quietude suggests little of its pompous past – pompous at least, I suppose, on the morning Catherine Parr left the small but impressive castle to become the last and surviving wife of Henry VIII. No doubt before embarking on that somewhat perilous course she knelt in the castle chapel, which now serves as Snape parish church, though much of the rest is a ruin.

Snape itself has seen better – or at least busier – days. In 1811, when woolcombing was the staple industry, 616 people lived here, patronizing four inns and (perhaps as a consequence) both a poorhouse and a lock-up called the Black Hole.

Westward from Masham runs the lovely little tributary valley of Colsterdale, where the villages inlcude Fearby, Healey and Leighton. Between the park of Swinton Castle and Leighton Reservoir is a mock Druid's Temple, complete in every detail and said to have been devised by the landowner, William Danby, to help the unemployed.

Rejoin the main dale and follow the road past Jervaulx Abbey with its memories of the centenarian squire William Lorenzo Christie, who cherished and studied the abbey whose monks were famous as horsebreeders. A race-horse owner himself, Christie understood and respected the Cistercian brethren who once trod the cloisters here. And few men were held in greater respect than Christie himself, especially in East Witton, where, in living memory, some cottages round the long green were said to be rented for no more than a shilling a week. Here is Braithwaite Hall (1667), owned by the National Trust and, 500 yards to the south-east, the remains of a hill fort which may have been here before the Romans.

At Spennithorne across the Ure there was once yet another of those dales castles, though only faint traces now remain. The church, though, is very firmly present and its buttressed, castellated tower might well be mistaken for a fortification. Nikolaus Pevsner, in his *Yorkshire North Riding*, seems unaware of a feature that has won Spennithorne a mention in most books. Among all his painstaking catalogue of multi-scallop capitals and square abaci he makes no reference to the Russian cross surmounting the van Straubenzee family's vault in the church-yard. It was 'captured' from the military chapel at Sebastopol during the Crimean War. Nor does Pevsner mention the picture in the church which shows the golden cross falling during the fighting. Perhaps he disapproved: it seems a strangely irreligious act to commemorate in a church.

Near Middleham, with its castle and memories of the mighty Nevilles, we enter Coverdale, where Miles Coverdale, 'the first Protestant', was born in 1488. His translation of the Bible was one of the triumphs of medieval scholarship. Almost as remarkable, he lived four score years at a time when religion was one of the riskiest of businesses. Carlton, the chief village of Coverdale, was the home of Henry Constantine, the 'Bard of Coverdale', a local poet, whose house bears a tablet inscribed with some of his lines and dated 1861. Built in 1667, the house was occupied until recent years by the Constantine family.

You might well think little had changed here since Henry wrote his verses and prescribed homely cures for homely ills – like potato water for chilblains. He was the sort of benevolent eccentric who seemed to thrive in remote villages, and there are few more remote than this one, which shares the little dale with West Scrafton, reputed birthplace of Darnley, husband of Mary Queen of Scots, and Horsehouse, where, in the packhorse days horses were 'baited' (fed) on their journey from Kettlewell in Wharfedale to Wensleydale.

Back in the main dale of the Ure, we nod politely to Leyburn, the present capital of the dale with its five inns and its markets, before calling on Wensley, whose name suggests that it *ought* to be the capital – as indeed it once was and might still be, but for the visitation of a 'fearful' plague in 1563.

This is surely the loveliest village in a lovely dale. Its church is rich in furnishings, such as the reliquary where once reposed the bones of St Agatha. The great house here, Bolton Hall (built in 1678 when Bolton Castle became no longer habitable), is surrounded by a wooded park.

Across the river, West Witton sees the annual immolation of Owd Bartle, after a procession punctuated by a chanted dirge. It happens on the Saturday following St Bartholomew's Day (24 August). The village church is dedicated to St Bartholomew, but the Bartle who is burnt in effigy is no saint but, according to tradition, a mere pig-rustler.

If any building can be said to 'dominate' this part of Wensleydale, it is Bolton Castle, whose name is often confused (not surprising) with that of Castle Bolton, the village which grew about its feet.

Fred Lawson, who painted here, loved it – a good deal more, I dare say, than did Mary Queen of Scots. Brought to Bolton Castle in 1568 after her army's defeat at Langside, here she stayed for half a year, despite the attempts of Kit Norton, of Rylstone, in Wharfedale, to rescue her. His efforts met with the same ill luck that long dogged this staunchly Catholic family, some of whom perished for their part in the Rising of the North the following year.

Bolton Castle, says Pevsner is 'a climax of English military architecture. It represents a state of balance between the claims of defence, of domestic complexity and comfort, and of an aesthetically considered orderliness.' Perhaps, but its degree of comfort was not enough to prevent the Queen from trying to escape.

Richard de Scrope built this fortress at a cost of £12 000 (worth £1m today) to guard Wensleydale. He was one of an illustrious family which included archbishops, chief justices, barons and earls among a host of other luminaries. With its four corner towers little reduced by time, Scrope's monument looks today much as it did in the days of its power, despite its 'slighting' by Cromwell in the Civil War. Its commanding officer, Colonel Chaytor, had resisted the Roundheads' siege with great gallantry, and before they acknowledged defeat on 5 November 1645 the garrison force were reduced to eating their own horses.

Near Carperby, farther along the dale, medieval ploughing terraces, or lynchets, testify to antiquity, as does the market cross – only seventeenth-century, though the market charter was granted in 1303. The substantial Friends' meeting house would surely gratify George Fox, who preached his gentle message with white-hot conviction hereabouts.

I wonder if he had time to visit Aysgarth and admire the falls – Upper, Middle and Lower – which confer on that village such distinction as it possesses.

Near the church a steep hill drops to an old bridge, still narrow, though it was widened by John Carr in 1788, which affords a fine view of the Upper Falls, caused as the fast-running River Ure tumbles between its wooded banks over broad limestone terraces for about a mile. Public footpaths take you through Freeholders' Wood to the Middle and Lower Falls, where a viewing platform is provided for visitors in wheelchairs. Even the sure-footed need to proceed with care in muddy weather, though then, of course, the hazard is likely to offer the richest rewards.

The name Freeholder's Wood is no mere archaism. Though the

wood now belongs to the Dales National Park, the freeholders, mostly from Carperby, retain a common right to gather wood in what is one of England's largest remaining hazel coppices. Not long ago I toured the wood with National Park officers who explained the mysteries of coppicing. The Park had begun a fifteen year programme, under which the trees, cut to just above ground level, throw up new shoots which will be ready for cutting in from seven to fifteen years, to be used for fencing. Year by year, two separate areas of less than an acre each will be coppiced.

No one could call Aysgarth the prettiest of villages, yet its visitors down the centuries have been legion. Some of their names and dates and comments are presented in the National Park Information Centre, which stands, along with a café and other facilities, on a hill rising from the bridge.

Listen to the diarist John Byng waxing dramatic in 1792 about the corn mill built by John Carr in 1784–85: 'a great flouring mill whose stream has drawn off half the water of the falls ... all the valley is disturbed ... rebellion may be near at hand.' Today, the old corn mill, after a varied career in which it has been ruined, repaired, burnt down and put to a variety of uses, is a museum of horse-drawn vehicles.

If it were not the mill, it was the railway that raised temperatures in what now seems the most peaceful of spots. The Victorian elite, as they doubtless considered themselves, who wished to keep Aysgarth secure against defilement, rose in protest when it was proposed to build a viaduct ... 'so ruining for ever one of the most exquisite landscapes in England', thundered a member of the Aysgarth Defence Association, which included such luminaries as Ruskin and Ouida, a best-selling novelist of the late nineteenth century.

Despite these high-minded protests, the railway came to Aysgarth; but the station, which no doubt reduced such sensitive souls almost to apoplexy, is now closed.

From Aysgarth it is not far to West Burton, secret village in a hidden dale named Walden. Here are all the charms that summon tourists, though few find them. On the vast green, which in term time forms the loveliest of school playgrounds, untethered horses snicker and crop the grass around the quaint market 'cross', a tapering spire reached by five steps and once surmounted by a weather cock which, some say, was decorated with ribbons on bygone feast days and carried round the houses. There is still a weather-vane on the cross, but the original one now adorns the roof of a converted barn.

The cross is a clue to the reason for that outsize green; it is a relic of the days when West Burton had a bustling weekly market ... How long ago? Well, the cross bears the date 1820 but the market probably antedated it by centuries.

One of the greatest delights of West Burton – Cauldron Falls – is as easily missed as the village itself. A modest signpost points the way to where the Walden Beck (which rises at 2000 feet on Buckden Pike) rushes through a narrowed bed to divide in streams over great slabs of rock in 'step' formation, and form a stone-girt pool – the cauldron – whose crystalline depths reveal pebbles polished for aeons by running water. An old stone bridge spans the beck; remains of a sluice gate recall a mill race, but the mill building is now converted to flats.

West Burton's surrounding hills seem to conspire to hide it: to the east, Penhill (1792 feet), to the west, Stake Fell (1624 feet) while Wassett Fell rises 1505 feet to the south. West Burton was here before the Conquest, but to these massive neighbours, a millennium is a mere tick of the clock.

Books on English villages tend to disregard Askrigg, perhaps because it is not a pretty place, at least in the conventional sense. It might indeed be said to have a harshness in keeping with its name – which makes no concessions to euphony (its original form was 'Ashridge'). Askrigg folk mind their own business – and mind it very well. Take any age you choose and you will find them demonstrating inventiveness and industry. In the eighteenth century the names of Christopher Caygill, Mark Melcalfe or James Ogden made it famous for clockmaking, which became a virtual village industry to vie with the knitters who transformed yarn from a mill (opened in 1784 as a cotton mill) into caps and scarves and stockings. A cotton mill in Yorkshire? Yes, but by and large, Yorkshire remains wool country, and it was not surprising that the Askrigg cotton enterprise soon found good reasons for turning over to wool.

So the needles of Askrigg often enough clicked in time to the ticking of an Askrigg-made long-case clock, and if the clock were one made by Caygill, the villagers might raise their eyes to find themselves staring into those of the devil himself! For Caygill delighted to adorn his clock-faces with portraits of Old Nick, relieved now and then, when he was in a gentler mood, by the odd angel or two.

Askrigg fell victim to 'progress' when the construction of a turnpike road made Hawes, further along the dale, the leading market of Wensleydale. but the market cross, with its five steps, still stands outside St Oswald's Church. Close by the cross is an iron ring where bulls were tethered to be baited in the intervals of brewing and dyeing and the practice of other skills by which, along with knitting and clockmaking, Askrigg folk contrived to make a living.

You might almost think there was something in the Askrigg air that attracted the energetic to this quiet little town whose steep main street is lined with narrow, rather secretive three-storey houses. One such dwelling, that has taken on a new and fictitious life during recent years, is the 'Skeldale House' of the BBC television series based on James Herriot's books about the adventures of a Dales vet.

But Askrigg takes fame in its stride. It has, after all, been the home for many years of those most distinguished of Dales historians, Marie Hartley and Joan Ingilby. And until recently, in Malcolm Stonestreet, Askrigg had a vicar who would himself have served very well as a character in a television series about life in the Dales of today. He was a prime mover in the Askrigg Foundation which initiated a craft shop, a residential youth centre and a home for old people, as well as establishing bursaries to enable hard-up youngsters to visit Askrigg from the cities.

Cross the Ure and you are in Bainbridge. It will never be the same for me, this village, since the passing of old Jack Mecca (or Metcalfe, if you insist on correctitude). Admittedly, the Forest Horn still sounds there from Holyrood, in late September, till Shrovetide. And though young Alistair, Jack's great-nephew, is a worthy upholder of the tradition, those who knew 'awd Jack' cannot but miss him. Whether in his workaday clothes, complete with flat cap, or in the uniform he wore when blowing the horn on special occasions, such as Wensleydale weddings, Jack personified the dale itself.

Over a glass of Brown Ale in the bar of the Rose and Crown, just a few strides from his cottage, he would tell you the history of the custom which had been the prerogative of the 'Meccas' since time immemorial, perhaps since forest-keepers were appointed in Wensleydale during the time of William the Conqueror. Among their duties was the sounding of a horn to guide travellers crossing the fells during the perilous winter months. Nowadays you may travel the dales more safely than city streets, except at times of severe weather. But the sonorous note of the Forest Horn still wakes an echo from the sleeping centuries.

Bainbridge takes its name from the River Bain, the shortest in England, which overflows from Yorkshire's third largest lake, the legend-haunted, speedboat-pestered Semerwater. Countersett on its northern shore has a hall dating from 1650. And at Countersett John Fothergill, born in 1712 at a lakeside farm, Carr End, attended Quaker meetings long before he won fame as physician, botanist and philanthropist.

From here a twisty road will take you back to the main dale and Hawes, its westerly metropolis, famous for its tup sales, for the book shop founded by that archetypal dalesman Kit Calvert, and as a base for walking the surrounding fells. What names they have – Great Shunner, Stag Fell, Wild Boar Fell; flat-topped Addleborough was used as a summer camp by Romans stationed near Bainbridge at the fort called Virosidum.

Gayle, on Hawes's doorstep, bears Hawes no malice for having supplanted it in importance – or so the wiseacres tell you. Villagers, feeding ducks from the bridge, will gladly tell you what they know – and it is often a great deal – about this, one of the most photographed of villages due to its situation on each side of Gayle Beck, which swirls over great slabs of limestone creating waterfalls like Gayle Force and Aisgill Force.

Gayle's oldest dated building was erected in 1611, but there are foundations of earlier structures. And above the village there is a plateau which may have been the site of a Norse settlement. A quiet place, Gayle is dying, say some of its inhabitants, less than 150 of whom are permanent (as against the 'off-comed' holiday cottagers). Such transients value the peace of Gayle while missing, perhaps, the note of sadness exemplified in the local street called, 'Bachelors' Row'.

It is difficult today to reconstruct in imagination the Gayle of the historians with its pre-Victorian population of approaching 400 and its own 'gentry', whose names are still spoken with respect. These people had imposing houses and kept simpler dwellings for their servants. Yet not all the lowlier folks were servants or farmworkers: some worked in the cotton mill, built two centuries ago and later in use as a water-driven saw mill. Others were coal miners at Sleddale or in the quarries at Burtersett, like the father of the late Kit Calvert, the near-legendary cheese-maker, dialect expert and bookseller of Hawes.

Talk of quarrying reminds me that the cascading Gayle Beck is not entirely the unaided work of nature. Part of its original limestone bed was ripped out for road building, thus providing another example of the way nature, given time, can create new beauty even from man's disruptiveness.

When I was last in Gayle I was amused by a notice warning me not to camp, or even park, on Gayle Green. The latter offence, should you be tempted to it, is at least possible; the former would be uncomfortable, to say the least. For the only thing green on Gayle Green is its name. Instead of grass there is now concrete and asphalt. Gayle Green was, in fact, a casualty of World War II, its topsoil being removed to make a hard-standing for tanks.

Hardraw, north-west of Hawes, is famous for its nearby 'force' (waterfall) which drops a hundred feet into a natural auditorium where band contests, begun in the nineteenth century, have recently been revived.

Now we are nearing the end of Wensleydale. Not far from Hardraw is little Appersett (the suffix *sett* – a forest clearing – bears witness to its Norse origin) and, finally, Cotterdale. It hides at the feet of Great Shunner Fell (2340 feet) from which coal was once mined – by candlelight!

The essential Swaledale begins at Richmond and follows the course of the Swale from east to west until it reaches the source of the river, beyond Keld.

Richmond is no village but we can hardly pass by this enchanting, perhaps enchanted, town without at least pausing before its majestic castle keep, strolling around the enormous market place and reliving the past glories of the Green Howards in the erstwhile Church of Holy Trinity, now that regiment's museum. And how can I fail to mention the magical Georgian Theatre? Or Frances I'Anson, the Sweet Lass of Richmond Hill, whose short life was spent here.

The westward road through Marske to Reeth is one of the loveliest in Yorkshire. Here at Marske are Marske Hall, home of the Huttons for over three centuries. They produced two archbishops, one each for York and Canterbury. South-west of the village is an obelisk to Captain Matthew Hutton, who, when he died in 1814, was buried at his request on this spot. Marrick, across the river, still has the nave of its old twelfth-century Benedictine priory.

On now to Reeth, with its splendid folk museum housed in a former Methodist Sunday school. Here you can learn all about Swaledale's past, in which sheep and lead-mining figure in about equal proportions. The large green is surrounded by comfortable houses, and it all looks so solid and secure that it is difficult now to imagine the times – most recently in 1986 – when Swale's swirling waters broke out in flood to give Reeth folk the sensation of living on an island. Lord Wharton, who founded a charity to present Bibles to schoolchildren, obtained a grant in 1695 to hold a market here, whose start used to be signalled by a butcher shaking his apron.

From Reeth a road winds north-westerly through Arkengarthdale, whose stream, the Arkle Beck, flows from the bleak fringe of Stainmore Forest through this valley where lead has been mined since Roman times. This little dale's name dates back to an otherwise forgotten Norseman named Arkill, and the names of the hamlets of the dale have an equally ancient ancestry – Arkle Town, Booze, Eskeleth, Whaw. Langthwaite (which means 'a long meadow cleared from scrubland') is the largest settlement in this little dale. Its houses seem to huddle together for warmth and protection against the surrounding bleakness.

Half a mile above the village is the 'CB', an hotel so named after Charles Bathurst, who developed the lead-mining industry, of which all that remains now are a few derelict buildings. A fall in world lead prices in 1829 forced many small mines to close; the bigger ones struggled on till about 1880, when the cheapness of imported lead beat them too.

The road ahead takes us to Tan Hill, 'the highest inn in England', lost in a vastness of moorland. But our own village trail takes us back to Reeth, then westward again, by way of Healaugh, Feetham and Gunnerside (where Gunner, a Viking chieftain settled) to Muker, which, with its companions Thwaite and Keld has been said to make up the best trio of villages in all the Dales.

First, though, we move a little south of Reeth, to Grinton, with its church called the 'cathedral of the Dales', once the centre of one of the largest parishes in England. Because of the great distances between churches in past centuries, Grinton stood at the end of the 'Corpse Way', the route by which bodies were taken in wicker baskets for burial in what was then the only available consecrated ground. The journey could take two days or more, depending on the weather.

Grinton's broad, low, beautifully-sited Perpendicular church is a history in stone of the Dales, with its leper's squint and twelfth-century font. Both church and village were at one time a centre of Swaledale life. So many came here to worship that a weekly fair was once held here on Sundays, a convenient combination of the interests of God and mammon.

Muker's first church was built about 1580, as a thatched chapel of ease in Grinton parish with a burial ground to save the legs of mourners who would otherwise have had to bear their dead along the Corpse Way to the mother church. Isolated though it remains, Muker is remarkably self-contained, with all the usual village amenities, plus a recently revived local industry, hand-knitting, using the wool of the famous black-faced Swaledale sheep.

Through the little village school here passed the naturalist brothers Cherry and Richard Kearton, whose names are proudly recorded in tablets on the outside wall. Cherry and Richard were born at the neighbouring village of Thwaite just over a hundred years ago: their name is perpetuated by the Kearton Guest House among the little knot of stone houses, once occupied by lead-miners, beside the fast-flowing Swale. What better birthplace for naturalists than this beloved village surrounded by the fells that seem as wild and lonely today as when Cherry and Richard roamed them in search of the wildlife that was their passion?

Keld next. Need I say that the Vikings gave it its name, which means a place beside a river or stream? This grey, stony village looks as if it has grown out of the fells. Only in Keld, you feel, could anyone have made up his one-man band – using rocks which, when struck, emitted each a different note. His name was Neddy Dick and they talk about him still. They remember too Edward Stillman, minister at Keld's chapel, who before he embarked on his 48-year ministry in 1789, was a wandering preacher. 'A faithful man', says his memorial in the chapel.

Ackworth cross and church

A corner of Haworth

3 *Bilbrough, where 'Black Tom' Fairfax sleeps*

4 *Kettlewell – 'a pleasant jumble'*

5 *Hubberholme*

Nun Monkton. Ducks on the village pond

Ripley Castle, home of the Ingilbys

8 Above Ramsgill, 'a magical miniature'

9 Left Churchyard and cottages, West Tanfield

10 Opposite above Kirkby Malzeard

11 Opposite West Burton – 'secret village i a hidden dale'

12 Opposite above
*Bainbridge, where the Forest
Horn sounds nightly*

13 Opposite *The beck at
Gayle*

14 Above *Hillside cottages
at Reeth*

15 Right *Bridge at Reeth*

16 Muker, 'remarkably self-contained'

17 Staithes: fishing cobles moored in Roxby Beck

18 'The neck-breaking descent' at Staithes

19 Staithes: the Cod and Lobster Inn

20 Goathland: St Mary's Church and farm buildings

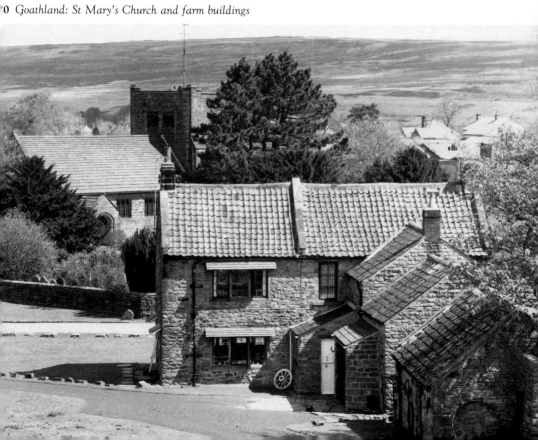

21 *The River Leven bisects the green at Great Ayton*

22 *The Friends' School, Great Ayton*

3 *Great Ayton. The building where Captain Cook first went to school*

4 *Kilburn: timber seasoning for the Thompson workshops*

5 Opposite above *Laurence Sterne [w]as rector of Coxwold, where the [fi]fteenth-century St Michael's Church [h]e knew still crowns the hill*

6 Opposite *Hutton-le-Hole: 'white [wa]ils, stream and hummocky green'*

7 Above *Thatched cottage at [T]hornton-le-Dale*

8 Right *Robin Hood's Bay: the 'steep [a]nd tortuous' street*

29 *Cottages at Flamborough*

30 *Four ducks on a pond . . . at Burton Agnes*

1 *White Walls are reflected in one of
ishop Burton's ponds*

2 *Church and cottages, Bishop
urton*

33 *Stamford Bridge – a great battle was fought here*

34 *Easingwold, north of York, in the ancient Forest of Galtres*

South from Staithes

BONNETS AND WHITE HORSES

Staithes is the most northerly village on the Yorkshire coast. Long ago the tourists discovered it, and in their wake those who cater for them. But the essential Staithes has remained distinctly and charmingly itself. The Staithes bonnets (like mob caps) worn on occasion by the women, are certainly not donned to titilate the tourists, though the admiration of visitors might well prove an encouragement. For 'Steers' folk are proud of their tumbled, sea-washed village, of its customs, its Fishermen's Choir and its associations with Captain Cook. He worked here as a shop boy in a haberdashery long ago washed away, along with at least one previous version of the village pub, the Cod and Lobster.

A guide to Yorkshire published nearly a hundred years ago, paints a terrifying picture of the 'break-neck descent' to the main street 'which is paved with the most attrocious cobbles' and 'without any apparent chance of escape, leads direct into the sea. The tiniest of bays has for its horns two broken cliffs – in the main, sheer. On the shore are bare-legged urchins and dead herrings – with the natural result of a fishy odour. Butcher's meat and "old clo" hang side by side . . .' Nevertheless, concludes the somewhat disapproving scribe, there is 'an air of prosperity' about 'this Elysium of primitive simplicity' which, he or she admitted, afforded choice subjects for the artist.

It still does, of course, and the present-day successors of Dame Laura Knight, who presided over an artists' colony here at a time when painters who followed their vocation on the Sabbath were pelted with fish-heads, often come here to live and work. But the prosperity reported in 1890 has sadly diminished, though fishing still goes on here, nets and lobster pots are mended outside red-roofed, small-windowed, white-painted houses. Colourful fishing cobles, their lines hardly changed since Viking times, are moored in the Roxby Beck which runs from Roxby High Moor between the guardian cliffs and into the sea.

Follow the coastline south now to Runswick, where cottages cling to the cliffs as tenaciously as any limpet in Runswick Bay. Divided by narrow lanes, bordered in summer by miniature gardens blazing with bloom, the houses appear almost to stand on top of each other. But their inhabitants apparently sleep peacefully, unafraid that a land-slip might cause a sudden mass removal, as happened three hundred years ago. A similar fate befell the neighbouring hamlet, Kettleness, in 1829, whereupon the uprooted villagers calmly boarded a boat lying at the foot of the cliffs.

A little way inland, at Lythe, the church has interesting relics and memorials though it was almost entirely rebuilt in 1910. At the foot of steep Lythe Bank, Sandsend is now a pleasant little resort giving few clues to the industrial past, but the clues are there for those who can spot them. As long ago as 1615 alum was mined here for the tanning and dyeing industries. The spoil, piled on Sandsend Ness, is said to have prevented the growth of much vegetation there. And the industry left other marks. But for alum mining, there would have been cliffs standing here which have long ago vanished.

A longer-lasting Sandsend industry, jet-mining, catered for the Victorian obsession for all things funereal, for this black substance was much used at one time for jewellery and ornaments. Even more recently there was a cement works here, but it closed in the 1930s and the sand castles which erupt daily on the beach manage perfectly well without cement until the tide comes in. A much bigger 'castle', along with remains of earlier structures, stands in Mulgrave Woods nearby; it was built for a natural daughter of James II, who married the Earl of Mulgrave.

Whitby, whose name is embedded in England's maritime and religious history, defies summary but hardly needs any. Its magnificent abbey ruins, its harbour and its memories of Captain Cook are surely well enough known to assure the village-seeker of whatever he needs in the way of diversion before venturing inland along the Esk Valley to some of the most delightful rural communities of the North York Moors National Park.

The A171 is our landward route, but we soon turn off this highway, to Ruswarp, with its working water mill fed at this point from a dam, which marks the tidal limit of the Esk. The seventeenth-century hall is now an hotel.

Nearby are Sleights and Ugglebarnby – surely one of the most cumbersome village names in Yorkshire – or anywhere else. The name indeed, which is almost bigger than the village, may well be as much evidence of antiquity as the round barrow on Sleights Moor nearby and the remains of two stone circles. The church (All Saints) in its present form goes back only to 1872 though its 'sumptuous' fittings ('elaborate and at the same time in good taste', wrote M.J.B. Baddeley in 1890) make it well worth a visit.

At Sleights in 1815 was born 'Flint Jack', who made a bob or two and a name for himself by manufacturing 'antiquities' supposedly discovered on the moors around, and selling them to collectors. On one occasion he even 'took in' the British Museum with a Roman milestone, all his own work. Was he, perhaps, driven to such naughty behaviour by a lack of excitement in his native village? Even Pevsner condemns Sleights Church as being dull inside as well as out.

Yet not everyone sought to flee from Sleights and its environs, though some may have wished they had. One such was the hermit of Eskdaleside, murdered by a local family in the time of Henry II. As a penance, a hedge (known as the Horngarth or Penny Hedge) is planted in the harbour mud at Whitby on Ascension Eve. But historians (who can be fooled, of course, just like museums) say it's all bunkum and the custom derives from the time when tenants of Whitby Abbey were required by the Abbot to keep their garths securely fenced.

Grosmont, south-west of Sleights, has a dourness not surprising in a village built for the sole purpose of housing railway workers. It was originally called Tunnel until, presumably, its inhabitants revolted and demanded the more mellifluous name based on the priory founded here in 1204 by Benedictine monks from Grandimont in Normandy. 'Tunnel', appropriately enough, is now the northern terminus of the North York Moors Railway. Planned by George Stephenson, the line was closed as uneconomic in 1965 and reopened to passengers in 1973 through the efforts of dedicated volunteers who continue to run it. A loco shed gallery certainly brings many to this village who would never otherwise see the place. Grosmont may not be pretty but it has great interest for the industrial historian. The mere thought of industry seems alien in these green and peaceful valleys, yet even Beck Hole, now famed for its woodland walks, was itself built to house workers for two blast furnaces. Also built, like Grosmont, for an industrial purpose, the village of Esk Valley, a little further to the south-west, belies its spacious-sounding name by being no more than a handful of cottages, once housing ironstone miners.

A school party was in Beck Hole and children scrambled among the stones of the 'hole' which surely gave the village its name. Darkened with tree-studded cliffs, the beck presents a striking scene which Algernon Newton romanticised when he painted the inn sign which still distinguishes Beck Hole's Birch Hall Inn. How many country pubs can boast a Royal Academician as their sign-writer?

Now that North Yorkshire has become aware of itself as a tourist attraction, the entire population seems to join in to describe local customs to the benighted incomer: quoits, for instance, which, a handwritten notice on the wall of the Birch Hall Inn explains, is still played on summer evenings on the green across the bridge. As each quoit weighs about 5½ lbs and the distance to reach the 'hub' is 11 yards, 'the throwing of the quoit is a test of skill, judgement and strength'. Twelve teams from the surrounding villages make up a league which plays on Mondays and Thursdays between May and August.

Goathland, whether its name is derived from the Goths or the gods, is one of the best loved villages in North Yorkshire. Set 500 feet above the sea, it rests amid the heaving, unchanging moors, a refuge, you could well believe, for ghosts of Roman and Vikings, bygone sorceresses and sober Victorian railwaymen.

The Romans, and not the giant of fable, made Wade's Causeway, the longest stretch of Roman highway preserved in Britain. From Wheeldale Moor it strikes coastward for more than a mile across desolate country which must have struck a chill in the Latin hearts of the soldiers who marched along it.

The Vikings, who followed them to settle and farm here, added their own words to the native Anglo-Saxon: terms like *foss*, which is applied to some of the family of waterfalls which join the bird song and the bleating of sheep to break the silence of this sun-dappled, cloud-shadowed plateau – Falling Foss, Nelly Ayre Foss, Thomason Foss, Water Ark and Mallyan Spout, which plummets 70 feet.

But the Vikings gave more than words to Goathland. It was their fertility dance, said to culminate in a gory execution, which became over many centuries, the 'Plough Stots' sword dance performed every year with cheerful dedication on the first Saturday after Plough Monday, though January snows lie thick upon the moor.

The Stots perform in summer, too, but it is the January dance that really matters. For it drives away evil spirits from the land and ensures a good harvest. Or so, at least, the Vikings might have told you. When the church converted the old ritual into a service of blessing the plough, the local plough-lads were loth to relinquish their bit of fun. So once the prayers were over they would drag their plough around the village, singing, dancing, begging money for beer – and ploughing up your garden if you refused them. They are better behaved today.

Witches once lived in Goathland, as of course they did everywhere. But here they all seemed to be named Nanny Pierson and to be possessed of such talents as transforming themselves into hares or shrinking small enough to walk freely and safely in a china cupboard. The witches have gone now from Goathland, but magic remains, not least in the presence of stream-driven monsters which ply on the North York Moors Railway between Pickering and Grosmont, stopping at Goathland station until the guard, with maybe a sprig of heather in his cap, whistles and waves it away towards Whitby.

In Goathland churchyard the dead, though doubtless colder than the living, are at least insensible to the chill of arctic winters which sometimes shut off this village for weeks at a time. A strikingly carved tombstone bearing Christian symbols catches the eye near the gate: 'In loving memory' (it reads) 'of George Wilfred McLane who went his daily rounds in the bitter winter of 1963, dying in parochial duty 4 March that year.' That is the sort of heroism Goathland honours.

St Mary's Church (which treasures a beautiful pre-Reformation chalice of silver with gold ornaments and a gold-plated rim, believed to date from about 1450) looks at first sight much older than its age of less than a century. Its architect, W.H. Brierley of York, was clearly an artist, 'Pleasant and unassuming', says Pevsner (of the church, not the architect). But surely Sir Nikolaus is faint in his praise, for St Mary's, low of tower and rugged of wall, seems perfectly suited to the moorland setting it has occupied only since 1896.

The first of its two predecessors was a small thatched chapel of ease associated with the 'Hermitage of Godeland', which began in the twelfth century when 'Osmund the Priest and his brethren' were charged to pray for the soul of Queen Matilda and 'to lodge and entertain the poor'. Far older than the church it serves is the Saxon or early Norman font brought here from Egton when the old church there was demolished in 1878; an ancient altar slab, possibly twelfth-century, found in the churchyard, is now set up in the north-east angle of the sanctuary.

If one function of the first church at Goathland was to entertain the poor, the village now welcomes any who can get there, by whatever means, even the abominable motor-bike. Still unquestionably a village, it yet possesses a surprising number of hotels, one of which, the Goathland, plays host to the Goathland Plough Stots dance team, whose 'swords' (strips of spring steel with wooden handles) hang interlaced over the bar fireplace in the 'Star of Bethlehem' formation of the dance.

In the parish hall, the Yorkshire Countrywomen's Association was holding a sale of clothes, cakes, plants and much-thumbed books. But the produce, though no doubt excellent, appealed less to me than the signs of Goathland's pride on the walls – behind glass in a frame, Goathland's War Record, happy photographs of the Silver Jubilee celebrations and an impressive collection assembled by some local geologist, of photographs of bridges, gates, houses, signposts, headed 'A Heritage of Stone in Goathland'.

August is the time to visit Egton Bridge a few miles to the north, for that is when the Old Gooseberry Society, founded in 1800, holds its show. Here are goosegobs such as you never saw before, as big as golf balls most of them and every one produced by a bona fide member of the society: for no others may compete.

You may try, if you're an optimist, to learn the secrets which have produced these giant fruits, but you are unlikely to succeed. Yet if you fade into the background and open your ears to the low conversations that fill St Hedda's schoolroom you may catch snatches of grower's lore – 'All this rain 'esn't 'elped. Ah keep an oomberella 'andy for 'em. They can have too much rain can berries!' 'Aye, an' they can 'ev too little,' another speaker weightily opines. 'When it's ower dry, Ah put a tin o' watter under a nice berry so as it'll get t'benefit o' t' ... what do yer call it ... evaporation.'

But the conversation is rarely more than perfunctory while the judging is in progress, whether the exhibit be a Lord Kitchener, a Princess Royal or a Prince Charles (the names bestowed on the varieties indicate the regard, nay, the veneration, in which the berries are held); or whether the class under the judges' eye is for the heaviest single berry, two berries on one stem or a group of 12. Not that these by any means exhaust the number of classes. The weighing of the exhibits is scrupulously performed, in drams and grains ('the smallest unit of weight', explains the Concise Oxford Dictionary of the latter, '1/480 of oz. Troy'). Useful prizes, such as garden tools and tea sets, reward the winners, and tea, to the music of a village band, rounds off the day.

Before the foundation of the Old Gooseberry Society, Egton Bridge's fame rested on its associations with Nicholas Postgate, the 'Martyr of the Moors', who was hanged at York when he was 80.

When I last visited the village, an exhibition in St Hedda's Roman Catholic Church recalled his story ... born at Egton Bridge in 1599, he had to practise his priestly vocation in secret, living at Ugthorpe just north of his native village but travelling over a wide area of the North York Moors disguised as a pedlar or gardener as he ministered to his scattered flock at the risk of his life. When a reward of £20 was offered for the capture of a papist priest the temptation proved too strong for the Excise man, John Reeves, whose betrayal of the old priest, as he christened a baby at Red Barn Farm, ended in Postgate being hanged drawn and quartered at York on 7 August 1679. Then Reeves drowned himself – or at least was found drowned at Littlebeck, near Sleights, in a pool where no fish has since been caught!

At Egton, close by, was born Tom Ferries (if he wasn't born at Lastingham, as they might tell you there). Tom left his initials on the Beggar's Bridge at Glaisdale and who had a better right to do so than Tom, who also added the date 1619? More than 30 years before, there had been no bridge, so he had been unable to cross the Esk, then in flood, to see his sweetheart and he vowed then that some day he would ensure that no other lover should suffer a similar fate. He made a fortune as a sea-going adventurer and returned to claim his bride and

build his bridge. As my century-old guide puts it, without attributing
the quote –

> And he built ere he won her, the bridge of his vow
> And the lovers of Egton pass over it now.

Lealholm, astride the river, has memories of John Castillo, poet,
preacher and stone mason, who may well have composed verses on
such natural delights as Crunkly Gill, hereabouts, a deep narrow gorge;
or the great flood of 1840; or he might have lamented the frivolity of
playing quoits on the green, an unfailingly popular summer pastime in
these parts. The house named Poet's Cottage was never occupied by
John but it stands on the site of his home.

Inevitably such a delectable spot caters for the tourist, with its craft
workshops and such, but if they help to keep Lealholm alive and in
good heart they are a small price to pay. And to balance the incursions
of modernity, Lealholm has ancient institutions like the Court Leet
which administers the riverside greens and other common land.

Who could write about Danby, a few miles to the west, without
quoting from the classic of Yorkshire rural writing, *Forty Years in a
Moorland Parish* by John C. Atkinson? He made the village and its
surrounding moors his life for 50 years, rather than 40. Having arrived
at Danby when he was 36, he lived there until he was 86, having in the
course of a full and many-sided life, married three wives by whom he
had 13 children. Where, in his list of achievements, he would have
placed these familial accomplishments it is difficult to say; but certainly
his other activities were evidence of an intellectual and social energy
that would have sufficed for three ordinary men. It took in its untiring
stride moorland prehistory, Cleveland dialect and the formation of a
local agricultural society which he ran as secretary for 32 years.

A factor in the success of his great book – he had written others – is
the unfading freshness of his observations. His roots lay not in the hills
and dales of 'Cliffland' (as Cleveland was called at first) but far away in
the southern flatlands of Essex. He was quickly fascinated by the wild
Yorkshire uplands, where the moors were dotted with the 'howes' or
burial mounds left by Bronze Age folk along with mysterious standing
stones and the medieval stones and crosses erected to guide wayfarers
at a time when to lose your way might imperil your life.

Atkinson's first arrival at Danby, his encounter with the 'minister'
and his first sight of the shabby, uncared for church, are described in
his book with a kind of shocked amusement. Equally revealing are the
casual reflections which bring to life past days in the Danby district.
'One might see an eagle in those days still,' he notes, recording his first
arrival at his future parish. Further along his route he met 'a stone-
waggon with a team . . . of no less than 20 horses and oxen attached to it,

half of either kind'. When he expressed surprise at a certain 'feckless' character who performed the duties of parish clerk and schoolmaster, the answer, 'significant as well as graphic', reflected both the humanity and the social economy of village life in those days: 'Wheea, he could do nought else. He had muddled away his land, and we put him in scheealmaster that he mout get a bite o' brëad.'

Cannon Atkinson's old church, restored in 1903 to its Early English style, stands two miles away from the present village, which gravitated to the main Esk Valley to benefit from the Esk Valley railway line from Whitby, surely one of the best scenic routes in England. But if there are now only traces of the village which used to surround it, St Hilda's Church has now, in the moorland, one of the most glorious settings in the world.

Danby Castle, facing the 981-foot Danby Beacon, is now used as a farm – and also by the Court Leet for their deliberations each October. It was probably built in the fourteenth century, like Duck Bridge, three-quarters of a mile from the village, which rash motorists insist on scraping as they try to negotiate its width of little more than six feet. This village offers a wealth of interest, but if there were no other reason for visiting, the Danby Lodge National Park Centre would provide one.

This being a book on villages, we must mention the one based on Botton Hall, near the head of the Dale and run by the Camphill Village Trust for handicapped adults. Visitors are welcome to browse in the shops selling produce from the community's farms and workshops.

No longer is there a castle at Castleton. The mound remains, but the stone is said to have gone into the building of Danby Church. Yet it retains its seventeenth-century inn, the Robin Hood and Little John. Westerdale, south-west of here, offers the monument erected in a cottage garden in 1727 by a sailor, Thomas Bulmer, as a thank-offering to God for saving his life when shipwrecked. Carved in rough capital letters all over the square main pillar is Thomas's life story. He found his final anchorage in the burial ground of Christ Church, where his gravestone bears a skull and crossbones.

Now we have left the territory of the Esk which rises on Westerdale Moor, for the land of the Leven. Lovely villages abound, like Ingleby Greenhow, where the church contains mysterious grotesque carving on the columns. Through Great Ayton the river takes its course, making a fine picture with the two village greens and the 'mini-mountain' Roseberry Topping reaching its pointed top at 1075 feet. They say that from this sublime vantage point Captain Cook, as a schoolboy, would gaze over the moors to Whitby as he dreamed his rolling, sea-sprayed dreams of the future.

Despite the encroachment of peripheral housing estates, Great Ayton remains for me as close to the perfect village as I shall find this side of paradise. One day, when I arrived to write an article about the place, I found my piece almost writing itself as the love of its inhabitants for their home village carried me along like a river of pride. The only aim of the folk of Yatton on that happily remembered day was to make sure I missed nothing in Great Ayton that was beautiful or interesting or memorable.

'Yatton', I called it, but its full name to the true inhabitants ('Yattoners', what else?) is *Canny* Yatton. And in this case 'canny' is given its true North Country meaning of bonny or engaging – not mean. I will have no truck with the old yarn that tells how Yatton folk once built a fence around their town and allowed visitors to enter only on payment of a fee. (Not that the idea is without its appeal to the sort of Yorkshireman who exists more often in comic send-ups of our county than in real life.) Nor indeed would there be any shortage of people willing, if they could enter in no other way, to pay the fee. For Yatton is as charming as its people.

The Postgate School, where Captain Cook was a pupil, is now a museum filled with relics of his travels. At one time the village had an even more evocative reminder of its greatest 'old boy': the cottage built for himself by Cook's father, who stayed in the village when his son went to work for a haberdasher at Staithes, then a considerable fishing port – sixth in England, no less. Perhaps young James saw the move as taking him one step nearer to his expressed goal – to sail farther than man had ever sailed before, as far indeed as it was possible to go.

The fate of that cottage is an embarrassment to Yatton today, as it is said to be, also, to some visiting Australians; for in 1934 it was dismantled and transported to Australia, there to be re-erected in a Melbourne park in celebration of the centenary year of the State of Victoria. But I need not dwell too long on a painful subject ... especially since there is so much in Great Ayton to be glad about.

Perhaps it would be overstating the case to call Yatton the Quaker village, yet the school here, run by the Friendly Persuasion, seems to have spread the spirit of good will through the whole village. I once had the pleasure of reading a diary kept by a master at the school in 1901/2, which presents school life as apparently an endless round of fun. Yet it was, in a sense, a claustrophobic world, 'a tiny universe' (as I remember writing) 'where a broken jampot in someone's luggage assumes almost earth-shaking importance and a brush with a local gamekeeper is described with enormous facetious gusto.'

However, on 2 June, 1901, the tiny peaceful world was invaded by a momentous event. As the diarist records, 'On Sunday at 10 o'clock the Boer delegate signed the terms of surrender ... Mr Arundel, with his accustomed generosity, granted us a free day, the more acceptable as this is an establishment where Friends' principles are taught.' In a journal clearly intended to be read aloud at intervals to an accompaniment of pupils' giggles, that was the only reference I could find to anything as serious as 'Friends' principles'.

The cottage built by Cook's father may be irretrievably 'down under', but its site is marked by an obelisk, and now the Captain Cook Museum exhibits a model of the house furnished as it would have been when Cook's father sat before the fire in old age looking forward to occasional visits by the son, who is commemorated, yet again, by a monument over a thousand feet up on Easby Moor.

In the churchyard of All Saints lie buried Cook's mother and her less famous children, who passed their lives more peaceably than James, 'massacred at Owhyee' (Hawaii), as the inscription puts it on the monument on Easby Moor.

Follow the western boundary of the National Park southwards to Osmotherley, the starting point of the Lyke Wake Walk, which takes you across the Cleveland Hills and the wild North Yorkshire Moorland beyond, to Ravenscar on the coast. Everyone knows that the distance travelled by the athletic zealots who complete the walk is 42 miles. What nobody has explained to me is why anyone, having found himself in this delightful spot, should be so keen to leave it. In me, at least, Osmotherley kindles more restful thoughts.

The Walk takes its name from the Lyke Wake Dirge, once chanted over the dead, who were presumed to be about to undertake a spiritual journey more perilous by far than that across the moors. At every point the soul is tested and its success or otherwise in safely crossing the moorland equivalent of the River Styx depends on the kind of life it has led on earth. Fail, and

> *Thoo'll doon, doon, tummle towards Hell's fleeams.*

Even today, religion is very much in the historic atmosphere of the village. John Wesley preached by the village cross, using as his pulpit the stone table on which market produce used to be spread. It would seem highly likely that he visited Mount Grace Priory close by, which is still England's best preserved ruin of a Carthusian monastery.

So dedicated were the brethren to the contemplative life that they avoided all unnecessary contact, even with each other. Every cell (complete with its own little vegetable garden) had a kind of serving hatch in the wall, a right-angled aperture which ensured that the brother serving the frugal meal was invisible to the recipient and thus did not distract him from his devotions.

Wesley visited Osmotherley 16 times in all, either because he thought his preaching was needed or simply because he liked the place. One result of his labours is the eighteenth-century Methodist chapel. Osmotherley is the setting, too, for an early-sixteenth-century lady chapel a mile to the north, restored in 1960 as a place of pilgrimage; and the Old Hall, where the Franciscans maintain a Roman Catholic chapel. There is a Quaker meeting house, for ecumenical good measure and the parish church, St Peter's, which stands on the site of a Saxon church, discovered when excavations were made during restoration work.

On my last visit, St Peter's, built by the same Carthusian canons who built Mount Grace Priory, was glorious with Easter flowers. They filled every available space. Even the umbrella drip troughs at each pew-end had been transformed into tiny gardens, while a table was full of miniature Gethsemanes made by Sunday school children. The service was over, the vicar and his wife on the point of leaving, but still with time enough to welcome strangers and talk about their church and parish.

I knew about the 'hog's back' stones in the porch with their chain plait carving that brought the Vikings to mind. Those stones were probably carved by wandering Danish masons who reached Yorkshire by way of Ireland. Dating from the tenth and twelfth centuries, such relics predate by half a millennium, perhaps, the fifteenth-century church, which may have had two predecessors on this site. I knew, too, about the font, which certainly stood in an earlier church. Indeed the pride of the vicar and his wife in the ancient, flower-decked church did not surprise me half as much as other flowers I had just seen in the spotless public lavatories, placed there, so the vicar explained, by the dedicated custodian of these conveniences. 'People come from far and near just to see them.'

Ryedale, now the name of a district council's territory, might reasonably be taken to mean the dale accompanying the River Rye from its birth on Whorlton Moor in the Cleveland Hills to Helmsley, a North Yorkshire market town metropolis complete with ruined castle, hotels and shops.

That original Ryedale is one of a beautiful family – Bilsdale, Bransdale, Farndale, Rosedale – constituting a large area of the North York Moors National Park. Their streams and becks, running from north to south in rough parallel, score the heathery heights and eventually empty themselves in the Rye before she joins the Derwent. The marriage takes place north-east of Malton, a sturdy market town with Roman origins, whose lesser brother, Old Malton, about a mile to the north-east, takes quiet pride in its parish church, formed from the nave of a priory founded in the twelfth century by the Gilbertines.

Northwards from Helmsley, the B1257 accompanies the River Seph through Bilsdale, passing the little village of Rievaulx, built largely of stone from the ruins of Rievaulx Abbey in the days when a roof over your head was more important than historical remains. The route touches Fangdale Beck, Grange and Chop Gate, whose name might be roughly translated as Pedlar's Way. In the old days the chapmen would travel the countryside selling small wares at remote farms and cottages and thus saving their inhabitants many a troublesome journey to the market town.

The road divides at Chop Gate, one branch leading west to Carlton, Faceby and Whorlton, where the gate-house of Robert de Meynell's castle still defies time and decay. At Swainby, the beck, crossed by bridges and delineated by white rails, runs through the village centre.

Here, in summer, notice boards tell of strawberry teas, guided walks and Women's Institute competitions. On a recent visit I found proudly displayed Swainby's score of 84 out of 100 in the Rural Village class of the Britain in Bloom contest. Specially commended were the 'well laid out' private gardens, the repaired pinfold and the maintenance of the new and old churchyards. But, the judges added gently, some painting was required here and there and the banks of the stream would be improved by mowing.

I'm not sure that they would, since this would regularly decapitate the wild flowers that find their homes there. In fact, on the whole, I'm more than happy with Swainby as it is, though the Church of the Holy Cross, which dates from 1877 looks rather 'new' for its surroundings. Its predecessor, now almost entirely a ruin, stands at Whorlton, half a mile to the east. The last normal service was held there on 7 March 1875. If ghosts walk, they should certainly be seen here any balmy midnight on the ramparts of the gatehouse of the church's neighbour, Whorlton Castle – looking out for the Roundheads whose target it once was.

On the waterside a display by the National Park authority tells you that the village of Swainby was originally laid out for the estate workers – swains – working on the estate farms of West Laithes and West Lees. Roman coins found here suggest that the village predates the Domesday Book, but of the original village, only the ruined church survived the Black Death.

For this reason, or possibly because of a more prosaic change in patterns of life and work, the population gradually migrated to the lower land along the beck, leaving the church and castle to keep each other company in old age, with only an occasional glance at the modern goings-on down the hill.

Back to Ryedale, which 'officially' means a grouping of towns and villages, such as Malton, Pickering, Kirkbymoorside and Helmsley, along with well over a hundred villages and hamlets. There are few pleasanter areas in England; a fact which, despite the efforts of the local authority and the Yorkshire and Humberside Tourist Board, is known to comparatively few tourists and holiday-makers, or life would soon become impossible for the natives. Yet tourism has probably proved the salvation of towns like Pickering, where the North York Moors Railway attracts many thousands of visitors who might not feel the superb medieval frescoes in the parish church, or the remains of Pickering Castle, were alone enough to justify a visit. The railway, first built by George Stephenson, closed by Beeching in 1965 and re-opened in 1973 through the efforts of a band of volunteer workers, offers a memorable experience as it traverses Newtondale Gorge.

Thirsk in the west or Scarborough in the east might both make a good starting point for exploring Ryedale. I suggest we travel seaward with the Rye itself. But first, Thirsk – a fine old town – may well detain us for a while, especially on a race day. Or if the sport of kings appeals to you less than the king of games, you may follow your inclinations to number 16, Kirkgate, the birthplace of Thomas Lord, who created Lord's cricket ground in 1787 at St Marylebone. Subsequently he removed its turf to Regent's Park and finally, in 1814, to St John's Wood.

And should you think that this is all a Yorkshire fable, go to Thirsk Cricket Club, where a plaque on the wall, presented by the MCC, bears witness to these hallowed facts. Thomas's birthplace is a museum now and by no means confined to relics of Thirsk's patron saint of cricket.

South of Thirsk, Topcliffe, perched on the eastern bank of the Swale, has a church worth seeing for its brasses and monuments; but our present journey takes us not to the Pennines but eastward to the Hambleton Hills and a small and unassuming village with one of the longest names in Yorkshire – Sutton under Whitestone Cliff. It rests at the foot of Sutton Bank, a precipitous incline which in former days struck terror into the hearts of all but the bravest motorists – or those with the most powerful cars.

Horror stories used to abound: there were drivers who could only ascend the one-in-four gradient in reverse, which must surely have induced a permanent crick in the neck or a compulsion to walk sideways for life. Nowadays, the ordeal is much less terrifying, while the view from the top, where there is a National Park Information Centre, makes the effort abundantly worthwhile.

From here may be glimpsed Penhill, far away at the gateway to Wensleydale; and, almost directly below, Lake Gormire, no doubt unwittingly passed while driving through Sutton. Few stretches of water hide themselves more successfully than this beautiful, somehow mysterious lake. To the knowledgeable its reputation is out of all proportion to its size, for Gormire is said by some to be 'the only true lake in Yorkshire'.

Just what Semerwater might say about that we can only guess. Each has its own mythology: Semerwater's is that of the sunken city from which sub-aquatic bells may be heard to chime, while Gormire is somewhat predictably said to be bottomless. But that fable is easily dispelled by the visible presence below the lake's surface of huge stones, which fell from the cliff above in 1755. The ubiquitous John Wesley (who should have been a reporter, for he seems invariably to have turned up wherever something of interest has occurred) visited Sutton soon after and recorded the inhabitants' impressions of these events, which no doubt provided the material for an electrifying sermon or two.

Kilburn, south-east of Sutton, has been called 'a village of school-boys'. There is an element of truth in that description, but it does less than justice to its subject. For Kilburn is also a village of craftsmen, in the tradition of that superb woodcarver Bob Thompson. And, if they'll forgive me for saying so, it is a village of supremely determined eccentricity, symbolized by the White Horse on Roulston Scar, a figure that, in spite of tourists and the laws of gravity and geology, this idyllic village strives to keep intact and – what is even less easy – to keep white.

I suppose the 'village of schoolboys' tag was earned by what the villagers might formally describe as their 'Feast and local costume frolics' in July. Not that they are much given to formality . . . excepting the mock formality which is the keynote of their frolics. I like to think that this annual 'feast' is really seen as an opportunity for the village to 'take the mickey' out of the municipal pretensions of larger communities; for perhaps the most popular event in a programme that includes horseshoe tossing and the inevitable foot race (to the White Horse, of course) is the 'Lord Mayor's procession through the village'.

His worship's coach is a gaily decorated trap drawn by a local lad, and lest you should be deceived by the gracious consort who sits beside him, dressed with a splendour to match his own topper and tails, let me assure you that both are men and that the 'lady's' striking figure owes quite a bit to two well-sited balloons.

As the cortege proceeds on its triumphal way, the chief citizen, whose election is for 'a year and a day', is more than likely to punctuate the proceedings with a rather arbitrary dispensation of justice, 'fining' whoever catches his eye for such unlikely offences as driving behind the mayoral 'coach' or displaying lace curtains in their front room windows. And the 30p or 20p fines imposed are willingly paid, for they benefit local charities. The Lady Mayoress, too, has her privileges, one of the most popular being the right to chase and kiss any pretty lass who takes 'her' fancy.

All this, with possible variations, has happened in Kilburn for nigh on a thousand years, though the White Horse itself can vouch for little more than a century of Kilburn's goings on. This famous steed's progenitor was, in a sense, the prehistoric White Horse of Uffington in Berkshire. This so impressed Thomas Taylor, a Kilburn-born man resident in London, who had made his pile as a dealer in York hams and bacon, that he felt that his own dear native village should have a similar ornament and set about providing one. He instructed the local schoolmaster, John Hodgson, to set his pupils the task of marking out on Roulston Scar the outline of a horse 314 feet long and 228 feet high. Then about 30 of the village men cut out the shape of the horse from the hillside turf and coated it with lime.

Alas for Thomas Taylor's optimism and good intentions, it was not long before the North Yorkshire wind and weather had eroded the dun-coloured friable surface of Roulston Scar, for without the turf and scrub which the village men had cleared, there was nothing to hold it together. The folk of lesser villages might have turned away with a regretful smile, but not Kilburn: it had set its heart on a white horse, and a white horse it meant to have.

From then on Kilburn had a purpose, a unifying determination to protect its very own symbolic steed, and keep it white in defiance of tourists and the very laws of geology! What did it matter if the Uffington White Horse was based on chalk, which was notably absent from Kilburn? Small problems of that sort were meant to be overcome, and overcome they would be, whether by means of lime, cement incorporating chalk chippings or the spent carbide bought by Bob Thompson in the hope that it might prove a means of preserving the horse's whiteness. As I write, an experimental use of white plastic is being considered.

Bob Thompson, one of three trustees appointed to administer a White Horse Fund, has probably shed more fame on Kilburn than the Horse, though this wood-carver of genius chose a much smaller animal as his signature. Working one day on the furnishing of a church, Thompson heard one of his workmen complain of being as poor as a church mouse. No doubt with a rueful smile, the not-yet-famous craftsman found himself almost unconsciously fashioning a mouse – whose descendants are now to be found on fine oak furniture in many parts of the British Isles. But they are often not found without a search. One place where you can hardly fail to find one is Kilburn's parish church, St Mary's, where they proliferate on pulpit, pew and lectern and where the Chapel of St Thomas was refurnished as a memorial to Thompson in 1958, shortly after his death.

But perhaps 'the Mouse Man' himself would choose as his memorial the library at Ampleforth College, nearby, where we shall soon arrive. 'My room', he used to call it, and he worked on it from the 1920s until illness finally forced him to cease from carving in the 1950s. His life indeed had been a love affair with the Benedictine school and Abbey, whose monks had commissioned him, whilst he was still struggling and unknown, to make a cross in oak for the churchyard.

Even today, as one looks around Kilburn, as neat and sweet a village as you can find even in North Yorkshire, Thompson seems close enough to appear, complete with moustache and flat cap, around the next corner, or in Mouse Cottage, where he lived and where today the work in oak of his heirs and successors may be admired.

Guide-book writers rhapsodize about nearby Coxwold and its snug situation in the Vale of Mowbray, between the Hambleton and the Howardian Hills. They delight in the way its honey-coloured houses, looking on to the velvet green bordering the long street, carry the eye to the octagonal tower of the fifteenth-century village church crowning the hill. They love its cobbles and its rooks, as much at home in the tall trees as wild geese swimming on the roadside lake next to Newburgh Priory. And well they might, for Coxwold is surely the most contented village in Yorkshire. What a place to grow old in, perhaps as an inhabitant of the Fauconberg Hospital, an almshouse founded in the later seventeenth century.

The Fauconberg Arms across the street must delight the many Americans who come to Coxwold and all too often depart, bearing with them, forgetfully, the keys to their rooms. Perhaps they feel a sub-conscious impulse to ensure their own return. This village exercised a similar fascination on Laurence Sterne, author of *Tristram Shandy*, who lived here at Shandy Hall, an odd, nooky house, and preached from the pulpit of St Michael's Church when he was Coxwold's incumbent of genius.

Before ever Laurence Sterne threw his sermon in disgust at his inattentive or slow-witted congregation, their forebears were doubtless mightily more excited by whispers of what was happening at the great house down the road – no mere rectory, but Newburgh Priory itself, home of the Bellasis family, whose magnificent tombs and monuments people the church.

It was the Bellasises, once landowners in Northumberland, who received the priory from Henry VIII, to whom Dr Anthony Bellasis was a chaplain and one of Henry's commissioners during the dissolution of the monasteries. Anthony himself never lived here, but left the property to his nephew, Sir William Bellasis, whose descendants have guarded well the secret of 'Cromwell's Room'. Not even Edward VII, when he stayed at the Priory, was granted his request to see what really lay inside.

It was Mary Fauconberg, Oliver Cromwell's daughter and wife of Viscount Fauconberg, owner of the house from 1647 to 1700, who, to save the Lord Protector's remains from desecration at the Restoration of the Monarchy, had all but the head secretly exhumed and taken inside the house to a tomb in 'Cromwell's Room', where they remain, presumably, to this day. It is said that the corpse of a lesser mortal, unnamed, suffered the posthumous hanging, drawing and quartering intended for the arch 'traitor'.

But the principal treasure of Coxwold is surely 'the medieval house where the modern novel was born', Shandy Hall, lovingly restored by the Sterne Trust. It was here, in a small study, that Laurence Sterne wrote *A Sentimental Journey, Sermons of Mr Yorick* and seven of the nine volumes of *Tristram Shandy*. This was the house loved by Sterne as his 'philosophical hut' and although he did not die here (but in London, of pleurisy, while visiting his publisher) his remains are believed to lie in the churchyard, in the shadow of the octagonal clock tower.

The story of how they came here seems strangely to echo that of the rescue of Oliver Cromwell's body by his daughter. Buried in a London cemetery, Sterne's body was presumably stolen by the 'Resurrection-ists' for anatomical research, returned to the grave, probably by Sterne's friends, recovered when the cemetery was cleared in 1969 to make way for flats and brought back to Coxwold by the Sterne Trust. With it came the memorial stone bearing a fulsome account of Sterne as *THE MAN, who with gigantic stride Mow'd down luxuriant follies far and wide.*

At the foot of the monument, a paragraph explains that it was 'erected by two BROTHER MASONS, for although he did not live to be a Member of the Society yet all his incomparable Performances evidently prove him to have acted by Rule and Square ...'

Somehow, I can't quite see Sterne as a Freemason, real or intending, yet his quirky nature might well have been amused at the thought of joining a secret society with elaborate and arcane rituals.

The ruined Byland Abbey, near Wass, has a dignity which suggests that it remembers well the time it sheltered a king. Byland began in 1134, when a group of monks, probably in search of a sterner rule of life, left Furness Abbey. For 43 years they wandered before they came here and founded what became the biggest Cistercian church in England. The king who found shelter in these walls was Edward II. He had marched against the Scots but his invasion attempt was thwarted, so he and his army headed for England.

At Byland, Edward felt safe enough to contemplate his next attempt, not knowing that Robert the Bruce was close on his tail. When the Scottish attack came it took the English by surprise. They held their own at the Battle of Byland until the Scots outflanked them, whereupon Edward had to quit the abbey and seek protection at York. He left behind much treasure, for which the victorious Scots never even thanked him.

An immense part of the charm of Ryedale lies in its monastic remains: not so much in the tumbled masonry itself as in the hardly comparable settings. If Henry VIII had never fallen out with the Pope, communities like Byland and Rievaulx might flourish still. Instead of being maintained by the Department of the Environment, the monks would spend much time organizing appeals for money to ensure the preservation of their ancient houses. Streams of would-be novices would queue to enter the hallowed doors so that they too could live in such delectable surroundings. The countryside, in fact, might be studded with Ampleforths! And had they all been as successful and notable as the Benedictine abbey and leading public school which shares the name of this village, the life of Ryedale might have been different indeed: it can hardly be mere coincidence that Ampleforth village is the biggest in Ryedale.

Ampleforth existed as a village long before the school that bears its name. Yet it is impossible to write about the village and ignore the community which has existed here since monks from France, fleeing the Terror, found refuge in 1802 in a house provided by Miss Ann Fairfax.

The brethren brought with them from their old home at Dieuleouard a number of cherished relics and around these they built their accustomed life of prayer, meditation and the education of boys, as ordained by St Benedict himself, the founder of the order.

There is about Ampleforth's monastic community that sort of happy humility which attracts notice without any conscious effort to court publicity. It welcomes the sort of visitors who might well have surprised those refugee monks from France. The most noticeable of these in recent years was none other than the Ocean of Wisdom himself, the Dalai Lama, the most recent incarnation of the Compassionate Buddha.

Did he long for his native Tibet when he gazed at the Rye Valley or explored the abbey church, in which Bob Thompson's mice hide among the woodwork? If so, he gave little sign of it as he beamed broadly on boys making their way to tennis practice and told them to study hard but to develop a warm heart as well as a good brain.

Ampleforth boys, despite the idyllic setting of their school, can never feel secluded from the world outside as long as such exotic visitors are welcomed within the walls, nor are the guests always eminent. Not so many years before the Dalai Lama's visit, 14 scugnizzi from Father Borelli's home for street urchins in Naples were guests for a month in the homes of College masters and village families.

Even without such newsworthy arrivals, however, Ampleforth would attract visitors – if only the numerous devotees of 'Mouseman' Thompson, whose life and work might almost literally be described as 'part of the furniture'.

Apart from the college (situated, in fact, in the neighbouring parish of Oswaldkirk), Ampleforth village – red-roofed houses bordering a long street – may appear unremarkable. A Quaker settlement once supported itself here by growing flax, and there is a partly Norman parish church, St Hilda's, containing an ancient effigy of a knight and his lady dating from about 1330.

Not far away is Gilling Castle, the Ampleforth College prep school. It is renowned for a magnificent display of glass, in a huge window of the castle's Great Chamber, that forms a heraldic pageant of the Fairfax family history. The glass and panelling were bought for the American newspaper tycoon William Randolph Hearst's home in South Wales and after his death were discovered, still unpacked, in London. They were sold to an antique dealer, from whom (in competition with Sir Billy Butlin, the holiday camp magnate) the then Abbot bought them so that he could restore them in their rightful home.

The castle also serves as the home of the Abbot of Ampleforth. That office was recently held by the present Archbishop of Westminster, Cardinal Basil Hume, who some years ago was strongly fancied as a candidate for the papal crown. With its strong Roman Catholic traditions, Ryedale would surely have expressed quiet North Yorkshire satisfaction if Cardinal Hume had been elected, while long-dead monks and abbots of Byland and Rievaulx and Newburgh would have risen from their graves to cheer.

Gilling has a strong claim to the affections of all true Yorkshiremen if only because of the interest taken in the village by one of the giants of cricket, an Indian prince, the Maharajah the Jam Sahib of Newangar, or, to give him his shorter and better known title, Prince Ranjitsinhji.

The Prince came to Gilling and what he did there reads almost like a story by Frank Richards set in the halcyon days recalled in the *Gem* and the *Magnet*. A one-time rector of Gilling, the Rev. Mr Borrisow, had been a tutor at Trinity College Cambridge, when who should have sat at his feet but Ranjitsinhji – and the former student apparently felt enough warmth for his former tutor to visit him in later years at Gilling. One day in 1908, the prince (or so we imagine) found the rector somewhat concerned by the need to raise £100 – no trifling amount in a small parish in those days – to repair the bell tower of his Church of the Holy Cross.

How the Prince came to his former tutor's aid has entered village legend. A two-day cricket match was arranged between the Yorkshire Gentlemen and the Prince's own team of immortals of that golden age of cricket, whose names are still evocative as Francis Thompson's lines about his 'Hornby and his Barlow long ago'.

Among the 'run-stealers' who flickered 'to and fro' on that Ryedale occasion were the Prince's friends C.B. Fry, of Sussex and England,

Test veteran A.C. Maclaren of Lancashire and the great Warwickshire wicket-keeper Dick Lilley. No wonder the Gentlemen of Yorkshire – amateurs against top professionals – were convincingly outplayed. Though it had rained on both days of the match, a total of nearly 2000 paid their entrance money to see Ranji's team, who batted first and scored a total of 361. Dismissed for 52 and forced to follow on, the Yorkshire Gentlemen had managed a mere 74 for 6 by the close of play.

So the bell tower was repaired, the money apparently allowing even for a clock to be installed. This clock the Prince was invited to start at a service of dedication. All apparently went as merrily as the proverbial marriage bell, despite the reported comments of one scandalized Christian at the spectacle of 'a heathen' starting *their* church clock!

Many years ago I lunched at Hovingham Hall with Sir William Worsley, his wife and other members of that distinguished and popular family. Hovingham had still to become headline news through the marriage in 1961 of Katharine Worsley to the Duke of Kent, so its peace was still undisturbed. Fortunately the news hounds who descended in great packs to report the Royal Wedding, the first in York Minster since 1328, soon departed to leave the village to get on with its own affairs, like the occasional musical festivals or operas performed in the Italian-style Riding School. One such event, *Handel at Hovingham*, was based on the eighteenth-century Grand Tour of Sir Thomas Worsley, who built the hall (minus a south wing, because alas, he ran out of funds).

In the grounds of the hall there are the remains of a Roman villa, and – what could be more Yorkshire? – a cricket pitch which the late A.A. Thomson ('happiest of cricket writers', as someone dubbed him) called the most beautiful in England. All this, together with Sir William's own collection of water colours, was shown to me by the squire of Hovingham, then Lord Lieutenant of the North Riding. He is remembered as an example of the best type of country landowner – modest, cultured, kindly, whose family was his chief interest, followed by cricket, his old regiment the Green Howards and the land entrusted to him by the industry of such forebears as Sir Thomas, Surveyor General of the Board of Works under George III.

The road from Hovingham takes you to Malton by way of Slingsby and Barton-le-Street. These, both 'street' villages, follow a trading route once trodden by the Romans, later by Saxon and Dane before ever the present Wyville 'Castle' at Slingsby was built as the home of Sir Charles Cavendish, who fought at Marston Moor on the Royalist side.

The house survives the ancient quarrel, but only as a ruin. Its building was broken off during the conflict and with Cromwell's victory the Cavendishes lost their lands, to regain them with the Restoration. Yet for some reason the house was never finished and left a victim to the slow forces of decay.

In Slingsby church there rests in effigy a knight in chain mail who may well be Sir William Wyville, one of the dragon-slayers who apparently abounded in the area in bygone days. (North-west of here, at Nunnington there lived another, Peter Loschy, whose story – and it's a good one – must wait until we get there.) Sir William's quarry preyed on travellers on the road to Malton, which must have been as big a draw to the crowds – farmers, shoppers, holiday-makers – in those fabled days as it is today. The only dragons breathing sulphurous fumes that you meet on the Malton road nowadays travel on wheels, but how did these tales arise of monstrous 'worms'? Is it fanciful to believe that they may represent folk memories of survivors of the great age of reptiles? Or had the dinosaurs – as most believe today – all vanished (except in fossil remains and King Kong remakes) before man, even in Yorkshire, could become their puny adversary? No use asking Sir William – his stony lips are sealed.

Barton-le-Street has a church, St Michael's, which seems to have brought a gasp from Nickolaus Pevsner while not leaving him entirely speechless: 'a sumptuous small Norman church rebuilt without any restraint in 1871'. There are those, indeed, who say it was also rebuilt without any necessity: but it is generally acknowledged that the Victorian rebuilders, a Leeds firm, 'builded well', perhaps, indeed 'better than they knew', for they incorporated into the new building what is generally regarded as some of the best Norman carving in England, and if they found it necessary to fill the gaps with 'Norman' carving of their own, at least they meant well and, it must be admitted, did it well!

Even when driving, my late lamented friend Mark Bevan, of Pickering, fisherman, raconteur and versifier, could rarely pass a bridge without stopping to gaze over it or down from it. Freudians may make of that what they will: Mark, as a good journalist, knew what to make of his foibles – either a poem or an article. In the case of bridges it turned out to be an article, which he entitled 'Parapet People', and which described a species of which he was a prize example.

One of the bridges which afforded him particular delight was that of three arches which spans the Rye at the grey and orderly village of Nunnington, north of Hovingham, whose thoughtful eighteenth-century builder had provided embrasures by which pedestrian parapet people might safely protect themselves while pursuing their investigations.

Mark loved this particular bridge because from here he could gaze unhindered across the sleeping river to Nunnington Hall – part Tudor, part Stuart – the manor house whose west wing dates from 1580, though most of the house was built a century or so later. The hall is now cherished by the National Trust and itself provides a home for the bewitching Carlisle Collection of miniature rooms.

Nonni, an Anglo-Saxon settler, first built his homestead on the site of the present hall, whose history is as chequered as its architecture is varied. William the Conqueror took the house and lands from the Sheriff of Lincolnshire, one Maerlswegen, and bestowed them on his own half-brother, Count Robert de Mortain. The property passed to the Abbot of St Mary's York, then through various hands into possession of the Grene family, which produced Mathilda, wife of Thomas Parr of Kendal – father of Catherine Parr.

Those were indeed turbulent times, Catherine's brother William, created Marquis of Northampton by Edward VI, became involved in machinations on behalf of the brilliant but tragic Lady Jane Grey. Though tried, like her, for treason and condemned, unlike her he was pardoned: but he lost Nunnington to the sovereign, who leased it to a succession of occupants until 1630, when Charles I sold hall and manor to the City of London.

Something in the air of this tranquil old house seems strangely conducive to treachery. Sir Thomas Norcliffe, the third of that name to live in the house, raised a band of 60 men of the parish and witnessed their oath of loyalty to King Charles I on 6 March 1641 in Nunnington Church. The simple villagers must have been somewhat confused when they found their master and themselves on Cromwell's side and the hall commandeered to house Roundhead troops, no doubt in preparation for the siege of Helmsley Castle. As troops seem always to do, they left the house in a proper mess and Sir Thomas did nothing to help, for he stripped the house of woodwork and lead to furnish the house he was building at Langton.

In the best North Riding tradition, Nunnington had its monster and also, of course, its local dragon slayer, Peter Loschy aforementioned, whose ingenious defence involved the use of razor blades and the assistance of his faithful dog. You may find Peter's story, as I did in the church porch, while in the church itself is a knightly effigy which is not, despite popular legend, a tribute in stone to the village hero, but represents Sir Walter de Teye, who was Lord of the manor here until his death in 1325.

Sir Walter does not want for company, for other of the great and noble have their monuments here, along with the jockey Thomas Jackson, who died in 1760. And if the 'dog' on which Sir Walter's feet rest is really a knightly lion, the church is not entirely without its dragon – or part of one at least – carved on a fragment of a tenth-century cross. There is much that is curious or otherwise worthy of attention in this fine parish church, with its Jacobean pulpit and seventeenth-and eighteenth-century plate.

Stonegrave, south of Nunnington, was the home of Sir Herbert Read, truly a Ryedale poet, for he spent his earlier years at Muscoates Grange, in the Vale of Pickering that was once a lake and more latterly a marshland. The amazing Sir George Cayley, whom we shall meet again as we near Scarborough, did much to make this land productive and habitable.

On the way to the A170 where we resume our journey to the coast, Harome, noted for its old cruck cottages, leads us to Beadlam, with its Nawton Tower, and, a little further north, Pockley, where thatched cottages are – or were – a feature unusual in Yorkshire. Kirkbymoorside, a richly interesting market town a little way to the east, gives access to Bransdale, punctuated by Fadmoor and Gillamoor, while at the head of the dale, almost lost in moorland, is the hamlet of Bransdale itself. Here, on the site of St Nicholas's Church, built about 1800, a chapel of ease has stood for centuries. Not that this implies great age in a setting where real antiquity is represented by the Bransdale Cairn on Bilsdale East Moor, erected by men of the New Stone Age.

Further diversions from the A170 will take you to Keldholme or to Appleton-le-Moors with its impressive 'French Gothic' church, Georgian houses and cottage lawns, very close to the much vaunted Hutton-le-Hole.

This, I must admit, is not my favourite village – though it is no doubt a favourite of many others. What, they might justifiably ask, is wrong with it? And I could reply with apparent perversity that nothing is wrong with it – it is in fact too perfect with its white rails, its sacrosanct hummocky green through which runs an unpolluted stream; its charming cottages and its general air of utter tidiness.

And yet there is something in this village for which I have only unstinted admiration: the Ryedale Folk Museum, a collection of early dwellings and farm buildings of the type once seen in this North Yorkshire valley of the Rye. A cruck house imported from Stang End demonstrates the old method of building farmhouses hereabouts by using a framework of beams arranged in the form of a series of three capital A's (the crucks), but A's with two crosspieces instead of one. There are other re-erected houses here, including two from Harome – an eighteenth-century thatched cottage with 'Yorkshire sash' windows and the former Harome Manor House, again cruck-framed. Another highly prized exhibit is a reconstructed furnace of the type introduced to Britain by Huguenot refugees in the sixteenth century. It was discovered on the moors in 1969, excavated, dismantled and transported – some of its stoves weighed over half a ton – to the museum where it was re-assembled.

Hutton-le-Hole steps back into its own past every year on a weekend in June, when a sort of belated May Day is celebrated. Children dance around the maypole and play ancient games – quoits, merrils, the bullring – while craftsmen and women demonstrate for admiring visitors such fascinating examples of timeless expertise as blacksmithing, lacemaking, corn dolly making, spinning and weaving, stone dressing, broom making, wood carving and coopery.

Lastingham, near neighbour to Hutton-le-Hole, seems a world away in atmosphere. The first sight of this village of red pantile roofs and warm yellow-brown sandstone houses usually awakens a joy which grows with closer acquaintance.

So many buildings help to spell out the village's ancient story. For instance, St Chad's Well or its companion named in honour of St Cedd. This last, with its stone canopy said to have come from Rosedale Abbey, stands by the green, a neighbour to Jackson's Bridge, which takes its name from a local R.A. John Jackson is also remembered, if hardly celebrated, for his attempts to remodel the parish church, St Mary's, in 1831 on the lines of a Greek temple.

Fortunately his well-meant improvements were corrected in 1879 when John Pearson restored the building. The church is rich in ancient stonework, but it hides its greatest treasure beneath it – the crypt dating from the eleventh century which was probably built to house the remains of St Cedd, the missionary monk who came to Lastingham in A.D. 654 to found a monastery. When he died of 'a pestilence', Cedd passed on his work to his brother Chad, who was soon called away to be the first Bishop of York and then of Lichfield.

For some years the monks of Lastingham carried the Gospel to the surrounding countryside and followed their simple rule of life. Then in 793 or thereabouts, Danish raiders – the same who ravished the parent community at Lindisfarne – apparently destroyed the work of Cedd and his brothers. It was born again, however, under the hands of monks from Whitby, who came here seeking a safer habitat than the coast afforded. Their first task was to build the crypt that houses Cedd's remains.

With its chancel, nave, two aisles and semi-circular apse, the crypt, which is entered today from within the church, is recognized as a great – in some ways unique – piece of early Norman architecture.

Sadly, its builders found no lasting home at Lastingham (though such was the derivation of the name). After little more than ten years they fled, leaving the monastery unfinished, to found St Mary's Abbey at York (now the splendid ruin which has provided a magnificent backdrop for the city's Mystery Plays).

Among the oldest buildings in the village, the Blacksmith's Arms, faces the church and here, two hundred years ago, the traditional village partnership of church and pub was carried a step further than usual, for the curate's wife was the landlady, while her husband played the fiddle there on Sundays. With 13 children to support and a stipend of only £20 a year he was no doubt glad of the extra pennies tossed him by the regulars.

Back to the main road now, by way of Appleton-le-Moors; but before long another deviation takes us to Sinnington, where a little medieval bridge on the large green seems to have lost its stream. Another bridge, dated 1767, still spans the river Seven. In the hunting season the quietude of this delightful place is broken by the barking and bustle of the famous hunt, which is at least 20 years older than that river bridge.

From Wrelton, further along the A170, a road by-passes Cropton, where there is a castle mound, to lead into Rosedale, another of the little dales whose present tranquility belies its industrial past. For in the last century there was a period of intense activity and great prosperity here due to the suddenly increased demand for iron, which had been mined in a primitive and desultory fashion for at least 2000 years. The population increased by more than five times and a 14-mile railway branch line was built, of which traces only remain today.

In Rosedale, long ago, stood a Cistercian nunnery of which little more remains than a few steps of a spiral staircase and the name of Rosedale Abbey village, largely built from stones which long ago sheltered the holy sisters.

We glanced at Pickering while attempting to define Ryedale, but we can surely justify a further mention on the grounds that this ancient and agreeable market town affords an opportunity to call at Levisham, where the parish had a forge as early as 1207. On Levisham Moor in the early 1960s was discovered an Iron Age smelting furnace in use before the Romans came, and probably five centuries before Christ.

Levisham can also be reached by a streamside walk through the Hole of Horcum, an enormous hollow in the moorland, whose origin is variously attributed to a giant, scooping up earth to pelt his wife, and to millennia of action by water. Whatever the cause, this is one of the most striking phenomena of the North York Moors, whether you soar above the Hole by hang-glider or are content merely to peer down from the A169 on the strangely toylike farms and animals far below.

Levisham stares across a gorge at Lockton, while between them, near a mill and a beck, stands a lonely looking church where a pre-Conquest gravestone is adorned by a dragon that might have snarled from the prow of a Viking longship. Pevsner calls the church 'forlorn'; and indeed, why *does* it stand alone, while Lockton and Levisham – now with another nineteenth-century church, St Giles's – seem to glower at each other over its head. Could it be true that a long-ago feud split a community that once worshipped there? A girl in a shop in Levisham told me she believed that a village that once rested in the valley had been wiped out by plague and rebuilt on the hill.

No such mysteries, as far as I know, cloud the history of Thornton-le-Dale, which has long claimed the title of Yorkshire's prettiest village. It is much loved by the tourists for 'cute' little bridges that cross the streetside beck to enable folk to reach their cottages dryshod. No Yorkshire village pilgrimage would be complete without a look at its hall, its almshouses of 1657, its much photographed thatched cottage beside the Dalby Beck and the church, which contains the effigy of a fourteenth-century lady, her head beneath a canopy. What could she tell us of the Thornton-le-Dale she knew? Perhaps this 'prettiest village' is not without its mysteries after all....

A small road branches off to the north-east and forks again. One branch joins the A169 which takes you back to Ruswarp, near Whitby, the other enters a thickly forested area dotted with villages such as Low Dalby, Bickley, Langdale End (with views of the remarkably conical Sugar-loaf Hill) and hill-top Broxa, scene of happy cottage holidays.

Born on Fylingdales Moor, the River Derwent travels south-east for ten miles or so, entering the beautiful Forge Valley after passing the scattered village of Hackness. Here the hall dates from 1791 and the church, St Peter's, has parts of an Anglo-Saxon cross recalling a nunnery which existed for nearly two centuries until Danish pirates descended on the poor sisters in 869.

From the Forge Valley the Derwent emerges between East and West Ayton, the latter being the site of a fourteenth-century castle. But there is still much of interest on the A170 before it reaches the Aytons.

Ebberston, a few miles to the east of Thornton-le-Dale was actually shifted to facilitate the hunting activities of William Thompson, MP for Scarborough and first owner of Ebberston Hall. Originally the cottages were sited in front of the house which now enjoys some fame as a miniature among Yorkshire's 'stately homes', of which it is surely the smallest. Rising only one storey above the basement, it was designed for Thompson in 1718 by Colen Campbell, who had a veritable mania for hydrostatics. He created the water garden, glorious with fountains, which was once William Thompson's pride and now, like him, is just a memory.

Perhaps the abundance of water was not an unalloyed blessing. One of the hall's most colourful residents, the great all-round sportsman George Osbaldeston, whose shade awaits us, no doubt impatiently, at Hutton Buscel, lived here in the first quarter of the nineteenth century and found the house too damp. He rebuilt part of it before apparently losing heart and selling it to the Cayleys, of Brompton, a few miles along the A170.

Here, at Brompton Hall, lived one of the most remarkable York-shiremen, the sort of all-rounder that flourished in his era (1773–1853) in the days before specialization put blinkers on genius. An inscription on his memorial porch added in 1895 to the large grey All Saints' Church describes Sir George Cayley as the father of aeronautics. Whether his progeny has proved a blessing or a curse depends on your point of view.

But Sir George did other things besides sending his sometimes unwilling servants for flights in his home-built gliders. He drained the 'carrs', former marshland in the Vale of Pickering (thus creating one of the most fertile areas of England) by making the Sea Cut to Scalby Beck and the North Sea, which relieves the Derwent of excess water in times of flood. He must have been a kindly man, in a generally callous age, for some of his most practical innovations were the result of his horror at the loss of life in disasters, whether on land or sea.

In Brompton Church on 4 October 1802 William Wordsworth married Mary Hutchinson, housekeeper for her brother Thomas, who farmed on Gallows Hill, near Ruston, just off the Scarborough Road. After the wedding, dutifully recorded by the poet's sister Dorothy, all three went off for a honeymoon to Dove Cottage, Grasmere.

Wykeham next, and Wykeham Abbey remains in my memory as the scene of a particularly high-spirited hunt ball. *Not* the sort of event normally held by nuns and indeed the 'abbey' is now a country house, though the Cistercian rule was followed here by a community founded about 1153. Part of the abbey still survives in the north wall of the village church, which is a bit of a rarity in that its tower, a relic of a fourteenth-century chapel, stands separate from the church, built in 1853, as a sort of gatehouse. The architect, William Butterfield, who built much in the North Riding, must have been quite a romantic. He also built the steep-roofed parsonage and the school, and so could almost claim the village as his memorial; there are certainly far worse ways of being remembered.

Hutton Buscel school, too, bears the Butterfield mark, as does the north aisle of the church, which contains monuments to the Osbal-destons, of whom George was certainly the most colourful.

Perhaps in our day he would have shone in the Olympic pentathlon, for though only five foot six, he was an amazing shot, as well as a splendid horseman and cricketer.

George, alas, has no resting place in the village that was his home for many years. He lies instead in Highgate Cemetery, having returned in later life to the capital, where he was born, ruined by gambling debts and cheats of one sort and another. Good fortune came late, when he married a woman who knew how to manage him and what money he had left. Until then, he had gone from one misfortune to another.

There is no hall at Hutton Buscel today. It was burnt down when George was only 21, and the kennels built to house his first pack of hounds are cottages now. It was after this fire that George moved to Ebberston.

A detour takes us to Seamer, where the annual fair is announced by a mounted man with two attendants. Three times he reads the proclamation out. Then the Lord of the Manor, or his representative, throws new coins to be scrambled for by the children.

Should you, as a stranger, still wait expectantly for the actual fair to start, tarry no longer – that's all there is! But at least any village child who has collected a handful of coppers is unlikely to consider it a waste of time.

Nor did archaeologists who spent their summer holidays a few years ago excavating a site at Seamer Carr consider it time wasted. There was a somewhat frantic air about this operation, for bulldozers were waiting to turn the 9000-year-old site, described as one of the most important in Northern Europe, into a refuse dump.

The area was once part of the enormous lake which during the Ice Age covered the whole of the Vale of Pickering, and because of the high water table on the carr land (despite the efforts of Sir George Cayley) the work could only be done in summer. The riches of the site consisted of flints and pieces of bone left behind by the men of the Stone Age.

The route north from Scarborough touches Scalby, Burniston and Cloughton, where a minor road hugs the coast as it goes by way of Cloughton Newlands to the ancient village of Staintondale. Here in the time of King Stephen, the first owners of Bell Hill Farm performed a duty (echoed today by the Forest Horn blowers in Wensleydale) of ringing a bell or blowing a horn each evening after sunset to prevent travellers losing their way. As recompense for this service the freeholders of Staintondale were granted, among other privileges, exemption from road and market tolls.

Close to Staintondale is Hayburn Wyke, a miniature bay, into which runs the Hayburn Beck. Here the Yorkshire Naturalists' Trust maintain a nature reserve rich in bird life.

A little further along the coast road, Ravenscar is the cliff-top finish point for the Lyke Wake Walk which began 40 miles to the west at Osmotherley. Here, in what is now the Raven Hall Hotel and was once Raven Hall, George III sought relief from mental illness and probably suffered more from the ministrations of a quack named Francis Willis than he had from his ailment.

Long before that time, a Roman commander, Justinianus, made his slaves or his soldiers heave and sweat to build a fort from which news of sea-borne raiders could be flashed along the coast. It happened probably late in the fourth century and Justinianus may have known in his heart that the days of Rome's greatness were numbered. But he ordered a proud inscription, claiming an 'excellent augury' and naming himself as builder, but never dreaming that holidaymakers passing a rainy hour in Whitby Museum might see his name and wonder idly who he was as they waited for the sun to re-appear.

The inscription and the foundations of the fort were found when Raven Hall was being built in 1774. According to some astute authorities, there may have been *two* eighteenth-century houses here, now connected, though even they are uncertain how to unravel the constituent parts. Not that guests in the hotel care much about that as they enjoy their golf along the cliffs, pausing between strokes to study the fine views over the sea.

Ravenscar sits on the southern horn of Robin Hood's Bay, which has nothing to do with Robin Hood, it seems, despite all those stirring legends of how, with his trusty long-bow, he cleared the sea hereabouts of French pirates. So his band of merry men never practised their shooting at Robin Hood's Butts, which are really prehistoric burial mounds; and Friar Tuck was never a Franciscan at Scarborough. Yet the legends are deceivingly detailed: when the French pirate ship surrendered, Robin seized 12 000 pounds of silver and vowed he would use it to build a home for aged sailors, though no trace of such a hospital remains.

Some say the name of the village arose from a confusion over the name Ravenscliffe. But it is easy to understand how Robin Hood might be welcomed as a kind of patron saint and honorary fellow townsman by the smugglers who used to lead the excise men a merry dance in this cliff-hanging maze of streets – one still named The Bolts – and cottages. Leo Walmsley, who lived and wrote here, gave 'Bay Town' yet another name in his novels – Bramblewick.

My guide-book of 1890 calls Bay Town (its local name) 'a fishing village of repute as far back as Leland's days ... a little cluster of red-tiled houses fringing the steepest, narrowest and most tortuous of streets. ... The shore consists of a belt of sands under the red crumbling cliffs...'. All of which might have been written today, though the fishing has sadly declined during the last century and many of the cottages once occupied by fishermen are now holiday homes. And there is now a 600-foot sea wall which will prevent houses ever again being washed into the sea – as two hundred of them were in two centuries.

6

Walking the Wolds Way

A CONGREGATION OF CHURCHES

Serious walkers may scoff at the gentleness of the Wolds Way, but it combines an agreeable tour of Wold villages with a virtuous sense of achievement. The 79-mile amble starts at Hessle (Hezzle in the vernacular) not far from that most magnificent of recent British engineering feats, the Humber Bridge.

By way of Melton, then Welton (with its pond and green, its church restored by Sir Giles Gilbert Scott in 1863 and window glass by Morris), the Wolds Way skirts and occasionally crosses the line between chalk and grassland – 'the grass so green', as the inscription reads on Jeremiah Simpson's headstone in Welton churchyard. Jeremiah, who died in 1719 in his 84th year, had 'eight times married been, but now in his ould age he lies in his cage under the grass so green'.

Twenty years after Jeremiah retired, full of years, to his 'cage' beneath the sod, John Palmer, alias Dick Turpin, was hanged at York. He frequented Welton's Green Dragon Inn, where he was eventually captured. Welton has charm, though it is rather too well manicured for my taste. A stream emerges from the ground to run, lagoon-like, beside the church and broaden into the inevitable duckpond. The church tower was in splints on the day of my visit. A glossy brochure appealed for £100 000 to make 'urgent repairs', and reminded us that 'Christianity was first established in this area after the conversion of King Edwin of Deira in A.D. 626 by Paulinus, chaplain to his queen, Ethelburga, whose parents King Ethelbert and Queen Bertha of Kent are commemorated in the large west window', the work of Burne-Jones.

Inside a gate at The Old Stables, water gushes out from a pipe in the wall. Nearby is a notice reading: *The ancient rights of users of the cattle well and overflow within the gates may be exercised at user's risk.*

Elloughton next, then the Way makes a sharp nor'easterly turn to Woldby before doubling back to Brantingham and the wooded

Brantingham Dale, whose steep, thickly wooded slopes offer a striking contrast to much of the open Wolds country. A fine old hall or two and pleasant cottages make Brantingham village a place to rest the feet awhile. And when they're rested I indulge my taste for village war memorials. Not too easy at Brantingham, where I had to climb over a chain to reach what Pevsner called the 'lovably awful' war memorial and read the names of 'the men from the farm and the forge and the mill and the fold'.

I know what Pevsner meant. The memorial was built from stones from the town hall which enshrined Hull's dignity in 1862, and, awful or not, there is a certain ingenuity in the way its components – like bricks from a child's toy box – have been assembled. Gateposts around the village stand adorned with urns from the same source and lend an amiable dignity to the scene, which has already a simple distinction due to the rustic timber porches on some of the cottages. But the Wolds is a fine place for halls, too, and Brantingham has its fair share in Thorpe Hall and Brantingham Hall.

At South Cave there used to be seven pubs. Now there are two – the Fox and Coney Inn and the Bear. There used to be a market, too, but now all that remains of it is Market Place and a grey, two-storey market hall surmounted by a cupola and clock and bearing the date 1796. Some call it the Town Hall, but its probable early function is evidenced by old meat hooks beneath the open arcading.

They say, predictably, that Dick Turpin passed through South Cave regularly on his way to York, dropping in at the Fox and Coney for a noggin *en route*. Maybe he was more popular here than in neighbouring Welton, for it was there, you will remember, that he was arrested.

Jordon de Cave owned much land here. He built a castle in about 1560 and there is still a castle of sorts – a castellated and turreted creation in yellow brick. Built in 1804, with a gatehouse added in 1870, it functions today as an hotel, sharing a sylvan setting with All Saints' Church. Tunnels, once used by escapers from an earlier castle, still exist, they say, beneath the placid grounds laid out in 1787 for one Henry Boldero Barnard, who rebuilt the original castle in 1791.

A copy of *Walking Round North Cave*, sold to me for 40p 'for church funds', enabled me to exchange nods across the centuries with previous visitors to South Cave's twin, including John Leland, who came here in the time of Henry VIII, and John Wesley, who in 1761 preached here 'to a deeply serious congregation, and was much refreshed'.

About ten years later, one Arthur Young came to Cave (as he called it) during *A Six Months Tour of the North of England* and was graciously received by Sir George Montgomery Metham, who had apparently found very little more when he came to his estate here than flat bog-land. However, reported the approving Mr Young, 'In a wood where there was once a paltry stream, Sir George has made a beautiful lake, and . . . has disposed on all sides numerous and thriving plantations.'

That lake is now part of Hotham Park, containing Hotham Hall, a more recent owner of which, Colonel Tom Clitherow, appalled by the human cost of defending the Ypres salient in World War I, erected his own memorial – a board on the gates reading 'Ypres 347 miles', and recording below the numbers of casualties.

Alas, Rita Redford, one of the booklet's compilers, gently doubted the story that Dick Turpin stayed here for a time between leaving Lincolnshire and finding his last brief home in York, where they hanged him.

Architectural antiquaries coo over North Cave door cases, which abound in Westgate particularly, their columns and cornices adding rural grandeur to the (generally) Georgian and Victorian buildings.

The Romans had a camp here and the Druids met on a hill three miles away, or so it is recorded by the indefatigable Arthur Mee, who also unearthed such local worthies as Christopher Ness, born here, who wrote a history of the Old and New Testaments and for his outspokenness was excommunicated four times.

Perhaps he joined the Quakers, members of which mildly oracular sect were noticed here as early as 1659 and were soon meeting weekly in each other's houses; hence Quaker Cottage, built in 1892 on the site of the old Meeting House. The Friends' burial ground has now become the cottage garden; those gravestones still visible bear simply the initials of the departed and a date.

North Cave has a Quaker Well (otherwise known as St Helen's Well), which was in constant use until 1937. Once, reports *Walking Round North Cave*, Quaker Well was a centre of village life and it quotes a rhapsodical newspaper report of 1894: 'Spring, summer, autumn or winter finds it . . . giving forth an inexhaustible supply. It is never frozen over in the hardest of winters. It is the friend of all . . . and so it will be found to the end of the chapter'. Perhaps the end of the chapter is not many pages away: piped water came to the village in 1937 and today not much of the stonework remains. But the Quaker Well is still worth a visit for the view afforded there of the village.

North Newbald hides itself, with its neighbour South Newbald, in a hollow of the Wolds. I recall the beautifully planted bank of the stream on Eastgate and the strangely named Gnu Inn with its sign depicting that beast so alien to the Wolds pastures. (Why a gnu, I wonder? Did it start life, perhaps, as The Gun? Or was it once the New Inn until a whimsical landlord felt like a change?) At the hostelry across the way, The Tiger glares in eternal frustration at the animal he would dearly love to stalk and eat.

Modernity has overlooked North Newbald. Its street names, The

Mires, Rattan Row, speak of the past. On Sunday friendly villagers greet you on their way to North Newbald's church of St Nicholas, the most complete Norman church in the Riding and one of the few built of an oolitic limestone which was quarried locally seven centuries ago: the stone for Beverley Minster came from the same source.

I first heard the story of Coifi, the high priest of Goodmanham, at junior school, a great place in those days for stories from Britain's heroic past. The details are a little vague now, but the fluttering of a sparrow trapped in Goodmanham's All Hallows Church was enough to recall the vivid picture that had remained filed in my memory for so many years.

The scene is the royal hall of King Edwin of Northumbria, whose kingdom extended from the Humber to the Firth of Forth. The king is in solemn conclave with the elders of his people, and the object of their discussion is weighty – whether to accept the new religion held by Edwin's queen, Ethelburga, and taught by her chaplain, Paulinus, or to cling to the age-old beliefs.

Edwin was already half-persuaded – more than half – by three incidents which seemed to him proof that Ethelburga's God was on his side. Had he not been saved from death by a friend who took the assassin's blow in his own body? Had he not achieved a great victory in battle, and had not his beloved Ethelburga given him a daughter? But the King knew that his people, too, had to be convinced. Hence the solemn council at which Paulinus outlined his faith in God's creation and the salvation of mankind through Christ.

A silence followed, for no man was eager to defy the old gods on whom doubt was being cast, or to risk the king's displeasure by speaking out in defence of them. Then a priest, too old to be readily afraid and for whom truth was the one abiding reality, rose to say that Paulinus truly spoke to his condition. 'Man's life is like the flight of a sparrow,' he said, 'that flutters from the darkness of a winter storm into the light and warmth of this hall, then, after a moment, flutters out, to where we know not.'

A murmur of assent greeted his words, but more powerful testimony was to follow, for it was Coifi, the High Priest himself, who spoke next. He had always known in his heart, he said, that the old faith was empty, but he knew that this new belief would bring not only fullness of life on earth but eternal happiness hereafter.

He borrowed a war horse and a battle-axe and galloped to the temple of Woden, where he flung the axe inside. Some of those who had followed him trembled, others shouted their defiance of the old gods, and, when no thunderbolts were hurled in reply, put torches to the shrine and watched it collapse in flames as the old faith died with it.

A few days later, on Easter Day, Edwin was baptized a Christian.

Some accounts say it happened at Pocklington, on his way to York; others locate the event at York itself. Wherever it happened, Edwin's acceptance of the Christian faith had far-reaching consequences for England and especially for York. For Edwin gave to Paulinus part of the site on which had stood the Roman headquarters of two centuries before, and here was built a wooden church, the forerunner of Europe's greatest medieval cathedral, York Minster.

The story of Coifi's destruction of the temple of Woden is told by the Venerable Bede in his *History of the English Church and Nation* (731) and the event is commemorated in Goodmanham Church by the 'Coifi window', which shows the high priest standing on a broken idol and brandishing a flaming torch. Tradition says All Saints' Church was built on the site of the very temple Coifi destroyed.

Long before Anglian invaders sailed up the Humber to occupy 'Godmundingaham' (as Bede called it), Stone Age people lived and died here, leaving evidence of their presence in the form of ancient earthworks and the burial sites called tumuli. Since men of all ages share much the same needs, it was always seen as a desirable site, south-facing, with springs of fresh water and no lack of building materials for dwellings.

Goodmanham no doubt suffered like many another northern village from the depredations of the Scots. As if the Scottish raids after the battle of Bannockburn in 1314 were not enough, the years 1315 and 1316 were plagued by non-stop rain which ruined the harvests, caused disease among the cattle and brought famine and discontent.

So when the Archbishop of York in 1328 took steps towards the repair and rebuilding of the church it must have brought new heart to the villagers and heralded more settled times.

Later centuries saw the church still further beautified. In 1530 the rector Robert Clevyng, and the clerk, Robert Appleton, bestowed on All Saints one of the most beautiful fonts in East Yorkshire, almost five feet high with a deep, richly carved octagonal bowl.

Of all the villages in Yorkshire, those of the old East Riding are most conducive to tranquility. And of all East Riding villages, is there one more peaceable than Londesborough, where the kings of Northumbria had the good sense to site their summer palace and where King Edwin met Paulinus on the day which ended in the destruction of the 'place of idols' at Goodmanham?

Today, in the shade of immemorial trees, goats graze the rough grass on the irregular green around which cottages of mellow brick seem to listen as boyish trebles echo from the church.

In the soft stone of All Saints the carvers of autographs have been at work down the centuries. TH, who left his mark here in 1767, did so only 32 years after the placing of the sundial above the door. In 1958 along came another TH whose work lacked the neatly wrought Georgian serifs of his predecessor, linked to him across the years by the pathetic human longing to leave a mark to be remembered by.

George Hudson, the 'Railway King', must have known such yearnings. He it was who bought the Londesborough estate of 12 000 acres from the sixth Duke of Devonshire in 1845. At the time, Hudson, the one-time draper's apprentice who was said to have wrapped all England in a net of steel rails, was planning the line from York to Market Weighton and with typical egocentricity planned it with a private station for himself at the edge of the estate at Shiptonthorpe, a few miles south-west of Londesbrough. From the house to the station he made a two-mile, tree-shaded drive and though the station has long since vanished, the vista may still be enjoyed from the roadside west of Londesbrough. I hope Hudson enjoyed his brief hour of glory, for his shaky throne was soon to collapse.

Nunburnholme, a little further along the Way, was once the site of a convent for Benedictine nuns. With its air of peace and the well-wooded surroundings of its white-walled, red-roofed cottages it must have seemed the perfect home in later years to its famous rector, Francis Orpen Morris, whose picture in the church reveals a gentle, melancholy-looking man. From 1854 to 1895 he ministered here, toiling between sermons and parish meetings, weddings and funerals, at his monumental *Natural History of British Birds*. The tower of his old church, St James's, opened in 1902, was built in his memory.

Nunburnholme's treasure is the thousand-year-old Anglo-Saxon cross shaft, best in the Riding, which came to light when the south porch of St James's was removed during the restoration of 1872–3. Marmaduke Morris, who followed his father as rector, described carvings of the cross in great detail, expatiating on the beasts and birds, weapons and helmets of Saxon and Norman times and speculating on whether a carving on the west face of the cross represented 'the head of a baby centaur being carried on its parent's back' or the detached head of a human victim killed by the centaur.

At the top of a lane leading to the village of Warter there stands an historic symbol of the life of the East Yorkshire Wolds. It is the winning post of 'the oldest horse race in the world', as we learn from one side of the arm pointing from the grass-grown verge. On the other side we read: *Kiplingcotes Derby 1519*. That date is the subject of some dispute, but there is no doubt that this rural race, run every year on the third Thursday in March, is an ancient institution.

The event itself is hardly part of the Warter story (it is described more fully elsewhere), yet it chimes with the village atmosphere as harmoniously as the bells of the slim-spired St James's Church. There is little else to be heard here, apart from the lowing of cattle and some quacking from the village pond of five white ducks which home in on the occasional visitor with faultless accuracy.

Warter's chief attraction for most is a row of thatched cottages with thatched porches, that look out on the war memorial on its green mound, dedicated 'to the men of Warter Priory Estate who fell in the Great War'.

The Warter Estate offices are here, but the priory itself has left only a few traces behind the church. It was founded for Augustinian canons in 1132, when there was already a church here, a Saxon foundation which, hidden in Warter's wooded hollow, seems to have escaped the attention of the Normans as they laid much of the district waste. The church was given to the priory and its canons provided Warter's vicars for many years.

Until 1972 there was a fine house here, frequently misnamed Warter Priory, though it was more properly called Warter House. Built in the late seventeenth century and extended in Victorian times, it is sought in vain today.

Better known than Millington, a few miles north-west of Warter, is the area of uncharacteristic Wolds country that shares its name – Millington Pastures. When ploughing began in the early sixties on land which had hitherto been used only for grazing, 300 dedicated walkers descended on an astonished Millington to protest and to re-establish rights of way. From such dedication was born the Wolds Way.

Huggate, a little east of the Wolds Way, is as unassuming as its name, a true Wolds village, chiefly concerned with crops and livestock. Hence the board in the church headed Manor of Huggate and dated 9 October 1826. This lists the names of a jury empowered to impose fines for such misdemeanours as suffering swine or geese to be in the streets between Old May Day and Old Lammas, or harbouring vagrants. The present village spirit is no doubt better expressed by a notice on the little pedal instrument in a corner of the church – 'the reed organ was presented to our parish church . . . by Huggate Methodist Chapel and is *much treasured.'*

At the side of the road to Fridaythorpe on Huggate Wold I found a piece of masonry somewhat quaintly inscribed

Petrol
5 furlongs
HIC OPUS EST

It was still puzzling me when I reached this rather uncharacteristic Wolds village 500 feet above sea level with its two large ponds on the green and its low, square-towered church of St Mary hidden away down a long lane behind some beech trees and a farm.

The only sign of life seemed to be a bird trapped behind the wire-netting screen protecting the church door. But Fridaythorpe is no deserted village, despite its proximity to Wharram Percy, where little remains of a once-flourishing community but a ruined church. I found it surrounded by an encampment of enthusiastic archaeologists who think nothing of sleeping in tents between leaning tombstones.

Like many abandoned villages – and there are over a hundred in the East Riding alone – Wharram Percy is a ghostly monument to human greed and callousness. Five hundred years ago, landowners on the Wolds realized that with the rapidly growing cloth-making industry, their greatest source of profit was wool, and decided that sheep were therefore more important than people. Villagers were thrown off the land to fend as best they might, while their cottages were left to decay.

A plaque, complete with diagram, explains that ever since the valley was settled by the Saxons, dams have been constructed across the valley to gather the water from hillside streams for a mill pond and later a fish pond. Today this water is part of a nature reserve.

Mapped out in the grounds are the sites of former buildings – water mills, two manor houses and peasants' long houses which accommodated animals at one end, people at the other.

The theft of lead from the church roof brought the efforts of countless builders and rebuilders to nought; the building crumbled and became unsafe for worship, and in 1949 it followed Wharram Percy into decay. Of the five villages which once composed its parish, now only Thixendale survives to display in its church a list of rectors and vicars from 1273.

St Mary's, Thixendale is yet another of the many Wolds churches designed in about 1870 for that strange benefactor and 'ecclesiolic' (if I may coin the word) Sir Tatton Sykes. The work of George Edmund Street, St Mary's forms, with its lych-gate, the vicarage and a school, a pleasing group in its agreeable valley setting. Small wonder that some would claim Thixendale as Yorkshire's prettiest village, a distinction to which there has never been a shortage of claimants. Certainly it is one of the most isolated, even more so at times of heavy snow, when it can be cut off from Malton, ten miles away, for weeks at a time.

On its journey to the coast the Wolds Way passes to the north of Wold Newton, where, in a field to the south-west, may be found a barely legible inscription on a brick pillar. It describes how, on this spot on 13 December 1795, 'an extraordinary stone' measuring 36 inches by 28 and weighing 56 pounds 'fell from the atmosphere', making a hole 19 inches deep and a yard across. It was eventually given to the Natural History Museum, South Kensington, and for all I know remains there.

Wharram le Street, a few miles further along the Wolds Way, is certainly no deserted village and its church, St Mary's, is intact. Its tower is reputedly the oldest of any Wolds church and contains Saxon work. Before either Saxon or Norman came, the Romans were here, and indeed the village stands in the path of a Roman road which ran from Malton to the Humber. Near here was once a Romano–British villa.

Coastward continues the Wolds Way through the Great Wold Valley, a shallow, widening trough which it is hard to believe might have been formed over the ages by water, for the tiny chalk stream that remains from those times looks all too feeble today for such a task. This is the Gipsey Race, which, rising between Wharram le Street and Duggleby, takes a somewhat erratic course, sometimes above ground, sometimes below, for 22 miles to Bridlington.

Duggleby is renowned for the presence, just off the main road, of a round barrow, one of the largest in Britain at 20 feet high and 120 feet in diameter, which, when excavated, revealed the cremated or buried remains of many bodies, along with the flint and bone implements of a bygone people.

The four villages that stud the way for the next few miles all have churches owing much to Tatton Sykes. The first two, at Kirby Grindalythe and Weaverthorpe, were restored at his expense, while Helperthorpe and West Lutton further along the route, were newly designed by the same architect, the famous Victorian, George Edmund Street. For much of my information on these four churches I am indebted to Philip Brown's notes on *Four Sykes-Street Churches of the Great Wold Valley*.

Kirby Grindalythe (if I may again inflict its name upon you) means the church village in Crendalith, which being in turn translated means 'on the side of the crane-valley', or so we gather from Domesday Book. Alas, there are no cranes here today, though on a long Wolds evening, the conjured memories of these and other ghosts of fur and feather add a melancholy pleasure to the scene.

Of the other three churches, St Andrew's, Weaverthorpe, has a sundial above the south door with a mutilated inscription in Latin stating that Herbert of Winchester, chamberlain to Henry I, 1108 to 1114, founded 'this minster' in honour of St Andrew. Minsters, which almost invariably originated in Saxon times, were missionary centres staffed by travelling preachers, monks or priests, who taught the faith to the heathen populace in the surrounding countryside. Perhaps some of their zeal, lingering in the Wolds atmosphere, influenced Tatton Sykes.

Near the end of the Wolds Way Hunmanby has an air of contented retirement, for what is now a large village was once a busy market town. Its old market cross still stands in front of the Hall, which has been a Methodist boarding school for girls since 1928. Here lived the

Osbalderstons, famous hunting squires, appropriately, since the name Hunmanby is said to have referred to a place where hounds were kept to hunt the wolves which plagued the Wolds. The church, All Saints, which dates back to Norman times and is mentioned in Domesday Book, once offered succour to travellers who had suffered from the animals' attentions.

Archdeacon Francis Wrangham ministered here in the 1800s. He was a great bibliophile who enlarged the vicarage in 1803 simply to house his books, collected often at great expense during travels all over the country. That greatest of clerical eccentrics, Sydney Smith, came here to borrow the Archdeacon's books; they must have been almost neighbours when Smith was the parson at Foston le Clay, near Castle Howard. Smith may have been among the bidders at the three-week book auction which followed Wrangham's death in 1842.

Perhaps because of their former remoteness Wolds villages have been breeding grounds for the colourful custom, the eccentric individual and the extravagant gesture – like that of one lord of the manor who, according to ancient custom, would trawl the sea between Hunmanby Gap and Filey, using a pair of horses and a drag net. Having ventured out as far as he could with safety, he threw a spear sea-ward to show that his rights extended thus far into the ocean.

The Wolds Way ends at Filey. It may not be a village in the usual sense, though Old Filey, with its odd yards and its old smugglers' inn, T'Aud Ship, complete with secret panels and hollow beams, has very much the air of a fishing village. And indeed, fishing still goes on here, though less profitably than in days gone by. Filey's most striking natural feature is the great reef of rocks called the Brigg, which juts into the sea for nearly a mile. Its origin has been variously attributed to the devil and to a dragon that left its skeleton here. The creature died after its jaws became glued together with Yorkshire parkin. . . Just another extravagant gesture?

'Flamborough Village', wrote M.J.B. Baddeley in 1890, 'has little interest . . . a reputed Danish tower . . . several fair inns and a little Temperance House, the North Star.' There was, of course, the church, St Oswald's, containing an inscribed plate to Sir Marmaduke Constable, who fought at Flodden at the age of 70. And there was a fifteenth-century road screen (very rare) and the Leper Squint on the north side of the pulpit. (The reason the 'squint' is inside the church is that originally St Oswald's had but a single aisle.) The 'Danish Tower' is a ruin remaining from 1326.

We could hardly expect M.J.B. to mention a medieval window, the oldest in the church, since it was only discovered during repairs in 1969. (Filled with clear glass it has leaded lights in the form of – guess

what? – a Viking ship . . . those Danes get into everything!) And he or
she wrote too early to be able to include the Fishermen's Memorial
near the Post Office, that commemorates three men drowned in 1909
as they vainly tried to save the crew of a fishing coble wrecked in a gale.

Flamborough Head was considered worthy of mention with its
North Landing, and Robin Lythe's Cave was apparently as much an
attraction a century ago as it is today. Under the lea of Flamborough
Head, Sewerby has an elegant eighteenth-century hall, now an art
gallery, containing a roomful of memorabilia of Amy Johnson, the
Hull-born flier.

Inland from Bridlington is Boynton with its hall, for long the home
of the Strickland family on whom rests the peculiar fame of having
introduced the turkey to Britain, in about 1549. The red-brick Tudor
mansion set in a beautiful park is now used as flats, but many
monuments in Boynton church commemorate the Stricklands. The
most striking is the lectern carved in the form of a turkey by Francis
Johnson.

When Queen Henrietta Maria landed at Bridlington from Holland
on 22 February 1643 with arms for King Charles I, she came under
bombardment from Parliamentarian ships. She took refuge at first in a
ditch but was later given shelter at Boynton Hall while on her way to
York.

At Rudston, west of Boynton, on 23 June 1898 was born the novelist
Winifred Holtby, author of *South Riding* and *Land of Green Ginger*. The
monument marking her grave in Rudston churchyard, an open marble
book inscribed *God give me work till my life shall end and life till my work is
done*, assumes a special poignancy when we remember that her life's
end came when she was no more than 37 and before *South Riding* was
published, to be judged best book of the year and win the James Tait
Black Memorial Prize for 1936.

Rising above the tombstones in the churchyard of All Saints is a
roughly hewn block of gritstone. The tallest standing stone in Britain,
at 25 feet nine inches, it is estimated to weigh 46 tons. Since the nearest
source of that stone is at least ten miles away, the first mystery must be
how it came here. If we assume that a glacier brought it we are still faced
with the puzzle of how it was erected – probably in the late Neolithic
period or the Bronze Age.

In the north-east of the churchyard is the monolith's 'little brother',
three feet high, which originally stood east of its larger relative and is
generally believed to be connected with it in some long-forgotten way.

Anglo-Saxon missionaries, bent on Christianizing the Wolds, had
no scruples about making whatever use they could of existing 'pagan'
monuments. Hence the towering stone became for them and their
followers a 'rood' (their word for a cross), which, combined with 'stan',

or stone, became Rudston. They may even have added a cross-piece, afterwards building a church as close as possible to the already venerated site.

Later ages saw things differently: the devil, they said, furious that a church should be built in which to worship his divine enemy, hurled a great stone spear at the church but failed in his wicked plan, either because heaven deflected his aim or he was simply a rotten shot.

The ghost of Anne Griffith rests in peace at Burton Agnes Hall, south of Rudston, where her skull has been built into the walls, nobody quite knows where. Anne was the youngest daughter of Sir Henry Griffith, who rebuilt the hall between 1598 and 1610, and his daughter can fairly be said to have fallen in love with her fine new home.

One day, while visiting neighbouring Harpham she was attacked by robbers and carried home near to death. In her delirium she exacted a promise from her sisters that some part of her would be allowed to rest 'in our beautiful home' as long as it should stand. But when she died, her forgetful family laid her remains reverently in the churchyard.

Soon, ghostly disturbances caused the family to have Anne's grave opened, to reveal her body perfectly preserved. But in place of the pretty face and hair she had worn in life, the coffin contained a fleshless skull! Remembering their promise at last, Anne's sisters took it into the house, whereupon peace returned to the hall – at least until what became known as 'the screaming skull' was removed or reburied, or even thrown away, as, down the centuries, it has been.

The result, always, of such violations of Anne's dying wish has been spectral pandemonium. But now that her skull rests in a wall (presumably) of the Great Hall peace at Burton Agnes seems secure.

The manor house which Burton Agnes Hall (long the home of the Boynton family) replaced still stands near the hall, north-west of which, entered by way of a dense archway of yews, is the churchyard where Anne Griffith refused to rest in peace. But these sombre reflections should not colour your appreciation of the village itself, which is a charming collection of white cottages whose colour matches that of the ducks on the large village pond.

There is certainly nothing sinister about the Gypsey Race, a charming feature shared by Rudston with other Wolds villages, such as Burton Fleming and Boynton. Even so, there is a teasingly magical quality about this chalk stream, one of a number in the East Riding which have the habit of appearing and disappearing due to springs caused by large underground reservoirs and acting on the syphonic principle.

North-west of Burton Agnes, Kilham is well worth a visit, and so is Langtoft and any number of other delectable communities. Just south of Burton Agnes, Harpham, where Anne Griffith was set upon, with deadly consequences, gave birth, centuries before, to St John of Beverley. In the spring, do children still gather primroses to adorn the railing around St John's Well in the village, saving some to decorate his tomb in Beverley Minster?

Harpham has another, more sinister well. The story goes that once, when archers were practising their skills as the law commanded, a drummer boy wandered from the butts, fell into the well and was drowned. Long after the tragedy, whenever a death was imminent in the local land-owning family the St Quintins (splendidly commemorated in St John of Beverley's Church), a ghostly tapping could be heard from the 'Drummer Boy's Well'.

The sweeping curve of Bridlington Bay is fringed by small towns and villages, such as Ulrome, where a lake dwelling was found in 1880. Here we are in Holderness, formed during the Great Ice Age, when glaciers packed boulders and clay against the chalk cliffs of the ancient coast of East Yorkshire, which ran from Sewerby to Beverley. This 'marshee contree', as Chaucer called it, stretches south as far as Spurn Head, Yorkshire's 'tail-end'.

Between the River Hull, as it journeys south to lose itself in the Humber, and the waters of Bridlington Bay, the towns and villages are no less thickly sprinkled than in most other parts of the old East Riding. I think of Barmston, where the Boyntons lived before moving to Burton Agnes after the Civil War. The Old Hall which was their home is now a farmhouse, but with a moat remaining to reflect its former glory.

Skipsea, a little further down the coast, might once have claimed the title capital of Holderness, for in Norman times it boasted the castle of Drago de Brevere. A Flemish adventurer, he was the first holder of the Seignory of Holderness, having been presented with it by William the Conqueror – along with the King's niece for a wife. And Skipsea has a Holy Well, which to the unenlightened may appear just a pond.

What the Ice Age gave to Yorkshire in the shape of Holderness, the North Sea is steadily regaining, a fact which may be observed at Atwick, where the stumpy remains of the market cross provide a barometer of erosion. In 1982 it was some 730 yards from the sea. Until World War Two the sea was 792 yards away. In 1786, when it was probably first measured, the distance between cross and sea was found to be 1050 yards.

Aldbrough beach has its share of beachcombers, for hidden among the sand are such semi-precious stones as amethyst (occasionally), amber (now and then) and, of course, jet, that peculiarly Yorkshire stone once known as Black Amber and still worked and sold along the Yorkshire coast, though never as profitably as in Victorian times.

Our route south takes us to Garton, then Grimston with its fine old house Grimston Garth, built by John Carr in 1781–86. Better known, perhaps, for his work in the West Riding and the Dales, he nevertheless included some East Riding properties in his prodigious output, one of them being Boynton Hall.

The bell which tolled from the now-ruined church at the deserted village of Wharram Percy is now to be heard from the Church of St Margaret of Scotland at Hilston, consecrated in 1957 to replace one that was destroyed by a bomb in 1941. At Tunstall, down the coast, the shore pebbles of which All Saints' Church is built seem destined to return within a few centuries to the sea from which they came. At Roos the church has a turret probably used in more hazardous days as a watch tower.

There is a magical charm in the melancholy of the Holderness coast which becomes oppressive if you have too much of it. So take the road inland from Roos to Burton Pidsea, where the cheerful village inn takes its name from a legendary race horse called Nancy, which in 1851 was beaten only once in 13 races. She received the sort of welcome on her victorious return from York or Chester that only a pop star could command today.

Wind your way by country roads across the broad rump of the Spurn peninsula to Hedon, which may not be a village in any strict sense, but is such a character of a place that it demands to be included on the grounds that once it *must* have been a village. And if you retort that most places could make that precise claim, I can only admit to being partial! What else could I be when I have been privileged to join the Commissioners of the Hedon Haven at one of their meetings at which churchwarden pipes are smoked and punch, made to a secret recipe and provided by the chairman, is consumed.

The commissioners' first forerunners were appointed in the eighteenth century, when the dawning of the canal age raised hopes that Hedon might recover some of its earlier importance as a port. They have triumphantly outlived the port that they were meant to preserve and now function usefully as a charitable trust.

St Augustine's Church has seen the town's rise and fall, for the building of it started late in the twelfth century, when Hedon was the leading port on the north bank of the Humber. No wonder it was splendid enough to merit the title 'King of Holderness'. This square-towered ecclesiastical monarch obviously merits a consort and we find her not ten miles away at Patrington, where the 'Queen of Holderness' holds sway. To reach her we take the eastward path along the A1033 by way of Thorngumbald, surely the most uncomfortable village name in Yorkshire, with its twin suggestions of thorns and gumboils, though the Norsemen from whom the name descends certainly had no such ideas when they named it. Keyingham, like Hedon, has seen days of greater eminence as evidenced by the relics of three market crosses and the considerable enlargement and rebuilding of St Nicholas's Church in the thirteenth and fourteenth centuries. An ancient settlement, this, like Ottringham, the next village along the way. If Patrington had not received the honour, Ottringham itself might claim to be the home of the 'Queen of Holderness'; for its Church of St Wilfrid is splendid even by the standards of the Wolds.

Yet having arrived at Patrington, you can have no doubt where the crown belongs, for to find a church like this in a village anywhere seems astonishing. It would do honour to any city. With its breathtaking, intricately decorated spire rising 189 feet from the centre of the cruciform building, its crocketed finials and rich but delicate carving, it must surely have a considerable claim to be the most beautiful parish church in all England.

Building began in 1310, was halted in 1349 by the shortage of money and labour caused by the Black Death, and completed in 1410, when its Perpendicular style was the height of ecclesiological fashion.

But why was such a queen among churches built here at all? The fact that two reasons are offered probably means that no-one knows for certain; but it is said that the Archbishops of York, who held the lordship of the manor from Saxon times to the Reformation, were frequent visitors, and for all Christianity's praise of priestly poverty, there has always been a somewhat worldly tendency to surround the Princes of the Church with the most splendid environment possible. A less cynical explanation is that in former days, Patrington, with its two markets a week and two or three fairs a year, was a busy and thriving place on the main route from the coast to the centre of Holderness.

Here again, the haunting memory of lost towns and villages of Holderness rises before the modern traveller; for until the eternally rapacious sea stole them back, there were here the port of Ravenspur and the ancient towns of Therlesthorp and Frismark to add to the Patrington traffic. From his 'priest's chamber' over the porch of Patrington Church, the sacristan who jealously guarded the church treasures could see travellers from these and other places who might approach any of the entrances of this lovely church.

John Betjeman said it was like a galleon sailing over the Holderness Plain; both Nikolaus Pevsner and Dr Cyril Garbett, a former Archbishop of York, considered its beauty hard to equal. And a far less likely connoisseur of churches, the much maligned Captain William Bligh, of HMS *Bounty*, found its soaring spire invaluable to navigation. That was in 1797 – eight years after he had made his historic 4000-mile voyage in an open boat at the whim of his mutinous crew. Earlier that very year he had put down another mutiny at the Nore (with what relish we can only guess), and now, while commander of HMS *Director*, the Humber guardship, he was engaged on a less troublesome task, but one which gave full play to his brilliance as a navigator. This was the charting of the lower ten miles of the Humber from Spurn Head to Sunk Island. Since the flat landscape provided no headlands or mountain peaks from which he might take bearings, he must have blessed the memory of the builders of the church spires at Ottringham, Keyingham and, loftiest of all, Patrington.

Even as I write these words an appeal is being made by Friends of Patrington Church and the Parochial Church Council for £¼m 'to preserve the Queen of Holderness for future generations'. Urgent repairs are needed to many parts of the building and – for once – the sea is not directly to blame. An appeal brochure frankly declares, 'We are a parish of only 1500 people with a regular congregation of only 50 to 60 communicants. The cost of providing adequate insurance absorbs almost a quarter of our income . . .'.

When Bligh was marking the spire of Patrington Church on his survey maps of the Humber, Sunk Island was truly an island, detached from the north bank of the Humber and not far from the middle of the river. Today it is a flat parish, never more than 15 feet above sea level, criss-crossed by narrow roads and drainage canals – yet another example of how 'the sea giveth and the sea taketh away'. But not all the blame or credit can be given to the sea, for the parish, created in 1831, stands on centuries of effort to reclaim the Humber siltlands for agriculture.

Sunk Island may be sunk in name only, but Ravenser, probably founded by the Danes, who landed here and set up their raven standard in 867, sank long ago. So did the port of Ravenserodd, but Spurn Head remains, despite the apparent efforts of the concerted rivers of Yorkshire pouring in unison from the Humber mouth, to wash it away. In fact its precarious situation is less real than apparent, for it is the erosion of the northern shore, combined with the constant warfare of sea and river, that keeps this narrow spit of sand in place.

Should this balance change for any reason, the tiny community of lifeboatmen and their dependants who inhabit Spurn would find themselves on an island; though that would probably make little difference to their solitary way of life. This is surely a 'village' without peer; for situated here is the only constantly manned professional lifeboat station on Britain's shores, with the vital task of watching over the safety of the Humber estuary.

Research has shown that such points are thrown up and then destroyed by the sea in 300-year cycles. And the chief reason why Spurn did not vanish many years ago is the fact that man has bolstered its defences for military reasons. But Spurn Point serves more than defensive purposes: its presence ensures the strength of the tide which keeps clear the deep channel used by ships sailing into Hull. If it were breached, the tide would be weakened and the channel would probably silt up.

Previous generations of Spurn folk made sure that the Spit defied the waves by half-burying thorn bushes at the edge of the beach. In no time at all a wall of sand grew up around this prickly barrage. Thus the old enemy, the sea, was turned against its own destructive purposes.

Take the B1445 from Patrington and you travel by way of Welwick, Weeton and Skeffing to Easington, where the famous 'imp' looks down from the tower arch of All Saints' Church, built, like much else here, of the rounded sea shore cobbles in a highly attractive herring-bone pattern.

Kilnsea, a few miles down the narrowing Spurn peninsula, is Yorkshire's most easterly village. Hard to imagine now that this was once, like Staithes or Robin Hood's Bay, a fishing village girt with cliffs and with a pub frequented by old salts. The old Bluebell Inn, now a café, was built in 1847, optimistically a mere 534 yards from the sea. Now it is less than half as far from the all-devouring waves, which last century swallowed the medieval church, replaced in 1864.

Meanwhile the remaining human inhabitants of Kilnsea share this loneliest outpost of East Yorkshire with the wild creatures for whom Spurn's lonely inhospitability to man makes it an ideal refuge.

After Spurn, the route from Hull to Beverley seems populous indeed. Cottingham, though almost swallowed by Hull, still glories in its nickname, 'the largest village in England'. With its market square, its memories of a castle and relics of a moat, it has not been entirely reduced to a 'community of residence' for Hull University. And if proof be needed that Cottingham has been a village it is necessary only to look back to the fourteenth century, when Cottingham folk in common with the then villagers of Hessle and Aulaby displayed a very village-like bellicosity and not only laid siege to Hull but combined to deny its citizens fresh water. Pope John XXII, no less, was persuaded to intercede and from the time his warning was received, in 1413, the villagers apparently behaved impeccably.

At Cottingham, academics predominate, especially in the neighbourhood of the Duke of Cumberland pub at the corner of Market Green and King Street. Even more plentiful than the dons are the ducks and the dogs, or so you might believe. The ducks consider themselves rightful occupants of the lake of Thwaite Hall, if not of this one-time manor house itself, now a women's hall of residence whose occupants are not surprised to be awakened at 5 a.m. by a quacking horde demanding food. As for the dogs, they are everywhere, except, perhaps, those parts of Thwaite Hall firmly controlled by duckdown.

Between Hull and Beverley, villages dot the landscape traversed by the little River Hull as it winds quietly towards the Humber. Skidby, on the eastern edge of the Wolds, is famous for the only working windmill in the Riding, which is also the last surviving complete tower mill in north-east England.

From here you can travel across the fields to Walkington, with its Dog and Duck Inn whose name recalls the happily bygone 'sport' of duck-swimming – a real crowd-puller in less-sensitive times. A duck with wings pinioned, so that it could swim and dive but not fly, was put on the pond to be chased by dogs. Today water-fowl are encouraged to visit the pond and he would be a bold man indeed who threw stones at them as in the old duck-swimming days.

Eighteenth- and nineteenth-century houses border the green of this single-street village. By the roadside are the remains of a cross which marked the limits of sanctuary from Beverley Minster. If you want to see how Walkington enjoys itself while remaining kind to ducks, drop in on the village at Hayride time, when everything in horseflesh from Dick Turpin's Black Bess to a Victorian ice-cream cart or a 1914 British Army General Service wagon is welcome to take part in an equestrian parade as it winds its considerable length through neighbouring villages like Bishop Burton, or delights the horse-loving East Riding crowds in Beverley. And all for charity.

A couple of miles north of Beverley, Bishop Burton rests in a wooded hollow, its spacious green guarded by magnificent chestnuts. There are two ponds: one a large crescent, the other, smaller one resembling a reed-fringed handful scooped from Hornsea Mere. White walls and red pantiles reflect in its placid surface. The village inn bears the hallowed name of Altisidora – a legendary race horse, winner of the St Leger in 1813.

With fine ecumenicalism All Saints' Church contains a bust of John Wesley, carved from an elm tree beneath which he preached on the village green. Perhaps every year, in late July, the founder of Methodism presides in spirit at an open-air service held on the green. There is a holiday air about this occasion, especially on a sunny day, for the hymns are accompanied on a magnificent fair organ powered by a steam engine.

Few villages in Yorkshire are of greater proven antiquity than Bishop Burton. Here, in about 1600 B.C., Celtic people buried their dead, leaving bones and ashes contained in urns which have been unearthed from the many graves or round barrows which prevent ploughing in the south-west of the parish. The Romans, too, were here as their coins and the remains of a Roman road have made clear: in 1721 two mosaic pavements were uncovered by a puzzled ploughman.

In about the thirteenth century the Archbishop of York had a palace here. Centuries before that, a Saxon earl probably held sway. His successors as lords of the manor included Richard Watt (owner of the great race horse Altisidora) who, having started as a stable boy, became rich as a sugar planter. Today the hall and estate are used by the Humberside County Council as an agricultural college.

A little way to the north is Cherry Burton, where well-built houses in traditional styles and the inevitable pond and smithy offer the best of both worlds to a new race of affluent village dwellers.

From Beverley to Great Driffield the A164 keeps erratic company with the River Hull on its meandering route, touching Leconfield, better known for its RAF associations – 249 Squadron was based here in 1940 – than for the scant remains of the great Percy family's home here. Scorborough, a mile or two further along, bears little resemblance to its seaside near-namesake. Lockington is as pleasant as you would expect of any village hereabouts. The church has a panelled south chapel decorated with 173 heraldic shields associated with the Estoft family, whose shrine it became in the early seventeenth century.

Westward across the fields lies Lund, much photographed, with its old market cross on a tiny green, its forge close by and the 'Cockpit Trees', whose name hardly needs explaining. Happily there are no blood and feathers flying here today.

South Dalton (south of Lund) has a unique claim to fame as the starting point of the Kiplingcotes Derby, 'the oldest horse race in the world'. (Remember Warter?) Local tradition holds that the race began in 1519, when the local gentry wanted to assess the condition of their horses after the winter. That is why the race is held on the third Thursday in March. This is possibly the only race in the world where the runner-up, who is entitled to all the competitors' fees, may receive more than the first-prize winner. However, the first rider home receives the Jean Farrow Memorial Trophy, which commemorates the first woman ever to win the race – in 1939. Since then female riders have acquitted themselves with credit. Every rider officially must weigh ten stone 'exclusive of saddle'. Should he or she weigh less, stones from the fields, carried in a bag round the waist, make up the difference.

At noon a white flag waved by a villager signals the start of the race from the old Kiplingcotes Station. The four-and-a-half-mile course over the rolling Wolds follows the path of a Roman road between Market Weighton and Middleton-on-the-Wolds.

Sledmere, village of monuments, is itself a memorial to the Sykes family of Sledmere House, a rich nest of innovators and eccentrics. The very setting of the place, at the heart of fruitful East Yorkshire, is a tribute. A classical temple near the gates of Sledmere House acknowledges the fructifying works of Sir Christopher Sykes, who won the title

'Reformer of the Wolds', but his son, the legendary Sir Tatton, Fourth Baronet, also made the once-barren Wolds blossom.

When first Sir Tatton saw the light
Our farms were in a wretched plight

wrote George Whiting in 1865. But Sir Tatton was famous not only as 'the Farmer's Friend', who discovered the fertilizing value of bonemeal – he had noticed that the grass grew better where his foxhounds had gnawed their bones – but as one of the 'three great sights of Yorkshire', the others being Fountains Abbey and York Minster. Like those great edifices, in appearance he recalled the past – he dressed like the eighteenth-century squire that he had always remained at heart, though when he died, aged 90, the nineteenth century was well advanced. Famous as a jockey and a pugilist, he would walk enormous distances in a few days to see a race or compete in one, and he kept no fewer than 320 horses at Sledmere.

Sledmere House, where Sir Tatton was born, was burnt down in 1911 and rebuilt from original designs. The park and gardens are by Capability Brown, but it is the interior that holds the greatest fascination, not least the tiled 'Turkish Room', reminiscent of a Sultan's apartment. This was added by Sir Mark Sykes, renowned for his oriental travels and, more locally, for his formation of the Waggoners' Reserve, from local farm workers who served with distinction in France in the First World War. Their exploits are recorded on a rather squat, pinnacled pillar by three tiers of carvings in a naive style.

Not far from the Waggoners' Monument is Sledmere's official Great War memorial (though it did not start as such) built by Sir Tatton Sykes, the younger, son of the Fourth Baronet, in 1900, in the style of the Eleanor Crosses erected by Edward I in memory of his much-loved wife Eleanor of Castile. Sixty feet high, it would be difficult to miss. Yet another monument, a tower on Garton Hill, was erected in memory of the first Sir Tatton (he that was 'one of the three great sights of Yorkshire') by 600 of his friends and neighbours.

The Sykes's doings have been wonderfully chronicled by Christopher Simon Sykes in *The Visitors' Book* (Weidenfeld and Nicholson), wherein we meet not only the Tattons, father and son, but, among others, the Dancing Marquis who delighted to dress up in the most extravagant jewelled costumes, one of which was reputed to be worth over £40 000, and forced his wife to sleep naked except for a king's ransom of emeralds and diamonds with which he adorned her nightly.

Tatton Sykes the younger was a hypochondriac who took his own cook with him on all his journeys to be sure of having the milk puddings he considered essential to his survival. He conceived the idea that he would soon die, and although he knew not the day of his demise, was sure it would happen at 11.30 a.m. In fact, he died at three in the morning in May 1913 at the Hotel Metropole in London. The management wanted to smuggle him out in a hollow sofa kept ready for such occasions, but his son Mark insisted that Sir Tatton leave 'like a gentleman'.

'All right,' said the manager, 'on one condition – that he goes in the middle of the night.' And so it was agreed.

The Derwent sees a good deal of East Yorkshire from its birth on the North York Moors to its death 60 miles away in the waters of the Humber. Villages in plenty accompany its tortuous course, which used to mark the western boundary of the old East Riding. An historic stream, the Derwent. Like its sisters Ouse and Humber, it gave entry to the Saxons who settled on the lower slopes of the Wolds in the sixth and seventh centuries and left their signature in village names like Flixton, Saxton and Ganton. The last is renowned for its golf course, while Ganton Hall, with its lovely parkland, seems all the grander when contrasted with the single-storey, whitewashed village cottages.

In West Heslerton's Church of All Saints, the ubiquitous Sykeses confront us from yet another laudatory inscription, 'Whoever now traverses the Wolds . . . cannot but extol the name of Sykes.' Present-day visitors who find this countryside too tame and tonsured might well remember that wolves roamed these hills and valleys long after they were extinct in most of England.

The least agreeably named villages often surprise us with their charm and this is certainly the case with Scagglethorpe. Neighbouring Settrington might be considered marginally more fortunate in this respect. Not that Settrington lacks charm, with the eighteenth-century Settrington House in its beautiful park, its beck and the Norman Church of All Saints whose Puritan vicar (commemorated by a brass) was ejected from his living after the Restoration.

Further downstream, another estate village, Langton, combines a musical name with a paradisal beauty. St Andrew's Church here dates mostly from 1822, but Mary Ingram, whose sober Puritan effigy rests within, died in 1656. The wife of Thomas Ingram, of Temple Newsam, she might well rest in peace beneath this adoring epitaph:

> *Readers with reverence approach this tombe,*
> *Here lyes A Pattern for the times to come,*
> *The glorious envy of her sex where all*
> *Virtues and glories were habitual;*
> *A wife as one would wish; be this her pride,*
> *She nere displeased her husband till she dyde.*

No doubt much of this stone village was rebuilt by Colonel Norcliffe, one of the family who lived for many generations in the village and whose hall at the east end of Langton bears on its gateposts the hounds which formed its crest.

On now to Westow, with its eighteenth-century hall, its cresset stone in St Mary's Church, which has a simple carving of the crucifixion on one side and 12 hollows for oil lights on the other. Or to Howsham, birthplace in 1800 of George Hudson, the Railway King. He enabled countless thousands to travel to a degree hitherto undreamed of before he reached his own earthly terminus no further away than Scrayingham, a few miles down-river.

After Buttercrambe, crossed swords on the map denote the occurrence at Stamford Bridge of an event in 1066 that proved seminal in English history. The mere name of Stamford Bridge takes me back to the classroom to stand again in imagination in the ranks of the Saxons as they faced across the Derwent the combined forces of Tostig, brother of the English King Harold, and Harald Hardraada of Norway, whose ambitions were focussed on York. The English were already tired. To face this new threat they had marched from Kent, where they had been guarding the coast. Yet after a day in which 100 000 men struggled in bloody conflict, the exhausted Saxons were victorious. They were not to know the doom awaiting them at Hastings.

But if medals were awarded at Stamford Bridge, Harold should surely have pinned an MM on the tunic of the warrior whose initiative must have won the day. At one point in the fray, a wooden forerunner of the stone bridge we see today was held by a huge Norseman whose broadsword allowed none to pass. Then a Saxon, having glided beneath the bridge in a commandeered swine tub, speared the Norseman from below through a gap in the bridge timbers.

The pub across the present, gracefully arched stone bridge is called the Swordsman. And the Viking on its sign, with his horned helmet and flashing sword may well be a tolerable likeness of the giant who held the wooden bridge here long ago. Not far from the pub the Yorkshire Ridings Society cocks a snook at Humberside with a sign defiantly reading 'East Riding of Yorkshire'.

Having crossed the bridge, you see the elegant bulk of the old corn mill, now a restaurant, sitting in the river surrounded by ducks which swim in and out of the mill's supporting stone piers and arches.

Visit Stamford Bridge if only to inspect the public lavatories with their murals of Viking and Saxon warriors and 'maidens' inspired by a local councillor as an alternative to the more familiar graffiti. A more sombre memorial may be found on a grassy bank, where a roadside stone carries, in the briefest of sagas, a bald summary of the battle in both English and Norwegian. Some say that relics of the conflict are still unearthed from the fields around, but they say that of every battlefield. . . .

South of here, Wilberfoss was once the site of a nunnery, but the quiet sisters are all forgotten now, whilst a family who long ago shared their village home is remembered through one of Yorkshire's most illustrious sons – William Wilberforce, who freed the slaves. Elvington, a few miles downstream, has an ancient bridge over the Derwent, and its church, rebuilt in 1877, an unusual timber belfry.

At Wheldrake, reached through the fields on the western bank, St Helen's Church has a stone tower dating from the fourteenth century, but the rest was rebuilt in brick in 1780. Entering it can afford a sense of delighted surprise, for this is a church where light reigns and not the 'dim religious light' that so often tries the eyes of visitors bent on reading inscriptions, like the one I found obligingly pasted to a board with a handle for my convenience. 'A large Georgian room', it calls the main building, which has an apse filled with large windows at the eastern end, through which trees may be glimpsed.

At Wheldrake Ings the Yorkshire Naturalists' Trust plays host to thousands of wintering waterfowl. Hospitality of a different kind was doubtless offered at Wheldrake by the Benedictines, only fragments of whose priory now remain. Further down-river six hundred acres of the 850 that make up Skipwith Common, with its variety of heath and pools, are leased by the naturalists from the owner of Skipwith Hall.

Skipwith's Church of St Helen is magnificent, though the elaborately metalled door, with what looks like a 'sanctuary' ring as handle, may be Victorian. A catalogue of vicars from 1245 includes the name of William Wainman, clearly a Bunyan fan, as evidenced by the windows illustrating *Pilgrim's Progress* which he and his family presented to the church.

Negotiating North Duffield, motorists are faced with this roadside warning: *Caution: Ducks crossing*, and a picture of the ducks for the benefit, presumably, of visitors unable to identify the species on the village pond.

Sitting on the A163 as it crosses the river-loving B1228, the rather quaintly named Bubwith has a church, partly dating from the thirteenth century, which contains a wooden funeral helm and sword which were once carried at funerals. Downstream, at Breighton, beloved of the boating fraternity, is a pub called the Breighton Launch which bears the affectionate nickname *The Breighton Ferry*. The real Breighton ferry was sunk by skylarking soldiers during the war.

Hemingbrough has one of the most magnificent churches in the East Riding. Its perpendicular spire is twice as high as the late thirteenth-century battlemented tower which supports it, yet the church, which reaches a total height of 190 feet, manages not to look top-heavy.

Perhaps it gets away with such eccentricity because of the air of wry humour that pervades so much of this marvellous building, with its gargoyles and quirky bench-end carvings. In the stalls is probably the oldest misericord in England, dating from about 1200.

East of the Derwent, at Wressle, the remains of a once-magnificent castle rise above the flat landscape recalling memories of resounding times. The quiet village we see today had its birth in the need to accommodate the staff of 'Henry the Magnificent', the fifth Earl Percy, for whose predecessor, Sir Thomas Percy, the castle was built in about 1380. Reduced now to two towers with, between them, the south range containing the hall, the castle looks rather like a child's toy on a giant scale. Yet in 1648 the Parliament, nervous of so redoubtable a fortress, ordered its destruction, all except the south side. And what Cromwell left standing was very nearly destroyed by a fire in 1796.

Barmby-on-the-Marsh is the last village on the Derwent's course before its juncture with the Ouse. With such a name it must recall Cornelius Vermuyden, who came to these parts from Holland at the invitation of James I. He was the greatest authority of his day on agricultural drainage and without him the village story of East Yorkshire would certainly have been different.

Vermuyden, who was prosecuted for flooding farmlands because his manipulations of the River Don caused overloading of the Aire, solved the problem by creating his Dutch River, a relief channel from the Don to the Ouse at Goole, where ships trading from Howden and river villages like Airmyn, Reedness, Saltmarshe and Whitten often waited for the tide.

Within a mile or two of Dutch River, Rawcliffe may be one of the few villages to have had a 'king', even if Jemmy Hirst was of no royal lineage and never wore a crown. He was certainly a king among eccentrics, whose fame spread so far beyond Rawcliffe that he was invited to visit King George III, whom he treated in back-slapping fashion, inviting His Majesty to Rawcliffe, where he would find 'as much good brandy as tha can sup'.

Further along the Ouse, at Whitgift, you might suspect that jocular Jemmy had had a hand in painting the numbers on the church clock, for instead of the usual 12 hours, here there are apparently 13. Or rather, time apparently jumps from 11 to 13 ignoring the twelfth hour entirely.

Around York there are so many delightful villages an entire holiday could be spent exploring them. I think especially of the area of the ancient Forest of Galtres, of Crayke and Stillington, Sheriff Hutton, Sutton, Easingwold. . . .

Nearer York there are the Poppletons, Upper and Nether. To the south-west are two other 'twins', Askham Bryan and Askham Richard, named after sons of the land-owning family Askham. The Grange at Askham Richard, once the family home, now serves as an open prison for women.

Bishopthorpe has been the site of palaces of archbishops of York for centuries. You may travel here by pleasure craft from York, while at Stillingfleet, further south, is St Helen's Church, nationally famous for its Norman porch. Lesser known is the most poignant village gravestone I know. It records the deaths of 11 carol singers from Stillingfleet, drowned on Boxing Day 1833 when their boat crossing the Ouse was fouled by the tow rope of a barge.

But that is too sad a note to end upon. Village life, on the whole, is a happy life. We should be grateful to share in it when we can.

SELECT BIBLIOGRAPHY

MALCOLM BARKER, *Yorkshire: the North Riding*, Batsford, 1977

DAVID BOULTON (Notes and introduction), *Adam Sedgwick's Dent*, Hollett and Son, Sedbergh, and Boulton, 1984 (facsimile)

IVAN E. BROADHEAD, *Portrait of Humberside*, Hale, 1983

ROBERT A. CARTER, *A Visitor's guide to Yorkshire Churches*, Watmough for Yorkshire Arts, 1976

NORMAN DUERDEN, *Portrait of the Dales*, Hale, 1978

ALAN FALCONER, *Rambler's Riding*, Hale, 1975

JOHN HADFIELD (EDITOR), *The Shell Book of English Villages*, Michael Joseph, 1980

PEGGY HEWITT, *These Lonely Mountains*, Springfield Books, 1985

ROGER MASON, *Granny's Village*, Peter Davies

HARRY MEAD, *Inside the North York Moors*, David and Charles, 1978

NIKOLAUS PEVSNER, *Yorkshire the North Riding*, Penguin, 1966

DAVID PILL, *Yorkshire the West Riding*, Batsford, 1977

MARGARET SLACK, *Portrait of West Yorkshire*, Hale, 1984

GEOFFREY WRIGHT, *The Stone Villages of Britain*, David and Charles, 1985

GEOFFREY WRIGHT, *The Yorkshire Dales*, David and Charles, 1977

GEOFFREY WRIGHT, *The East Riding*, Batsford, 1976

INDEX

Figures in italics refer to illustration numbers